PRAISE FOR DOUG MINOR

"More than anyone I know, Doug Minor is deeply committed and passionate about helping people achieve their financial dreams."

Scott Coady
Managing Principle, Sage Alliance Partners

"Doug Minor is absolutely the best in the business. His direct and efficient approach has turned many floundering deals into happily closed money makers. Every mortgage professional veteran, as well as anyone planning on increasing their closing percentage, must read Doug's book immediately. I will read this book many times."

John Cofiell
Owner, First Rate Financial Group

"I have had the privilege to know Douglas Minor for approximately 15 years as a friend and a business associate. Mr. Minor's professionalism is second to none and his upbeat positive nature is contagious. I am also impressed by his leadership skills and overall business acumen. He is the true definition of an entrepreneur."

Jerry Stone
Managing Director, Stone Search & Consulting, LLC

ANATOMY OF
CREDIT
SCORES

AN INSIDER'S KNOWLEDGE AND SUCCESS SECRETS TO OVERCOMING THE COMPLICATED CREDIT SCORING SYSTEM

DOUG MINOR

Co-Author Edward Jamison

Easy
Credit
Relief Inc.
Raising your credit score made easy

ISBN 978-0-615-38741-3

Printed in the United States of America on acid-free paper.

Contents

"Personal Freedom is never given.
It is always fought for and earned."

—Dan Sullivan

ANATOMY OF
CREDIT
SCORES

Introduction

In *Anatomy of Credit Scores,* you will find real insight into why having good credit alone may not be enough. Understanding how your credit is affected and what you can do about it is also necessary. The flaws in the credit scoring system can work against what you may think is logical. I have reviewed and repaired thousands of credit reports in a quest to identify these questionable credit scoring models.

Few of us realize that the way we deal with the challenges and risks associated with obtaining and using credit can have such a huge financial impact throughout our lives.

Just like an athlete has a coach or nutritionist to help increase their performance, *Anatomy of Credit Scores* will equip you with the knowledge and direction you need to attain the outcome you desire. Make no mistake that this will take some effort, but with your willingness to commit in making it work, I know it will be extremely beneficial to your life.

**"You Need to Remember, the More You Know,
the Less You Will Owe"**

1

What Is a Credit Score &
How Is Yours Affecting You?

Since you're reading this book, it's possible that you've recently been turned down for a mortgage, a car loan or a credit card and are already acquainted with the term *credit score*. If so, then you likely know that this simple 3-digit number is critical to your financial well-being and affects many aspects of your daily life.

WHAT IS A CREDIT SCORE?

The credit score is a number—an important one. It was designed to convey to lenders the kind of financial risk they'd be taking by having you as a customer. Think of it like a grade in school, only this grade rates you on how you have performed in your various financial obligations. Do you pay your bills on time? How much debt are you in? Have you kept your agreements on repaying loans in the past? What other kinds of financial or legal trouble have you had? By summarizing these considerations and more, the credit score becomes a quick and effective way for creditors to best decide whether lending you money right now is really a smart move, and if so, at what price.

WHAT ARE CREDIT SCORES USED FOR?

A common American dream is one of independence, entrepreneurship, and often homeownership. And yet few of us have the earning and saving capabilities to pay cash to buy a house or even a car, or to start our own business. Instead of settling for a lesser dream—like taking the bus, living in an apartment, or working for someone else all of our lives—many of us choose to borrow money to take on our larger aspirations and then pay those loans back over time. As a nation, we have come to rely heavily on credit to live comfortably and to pursue our goals.

Creditors and other lenders have only been too eager to help. Their revenue is generated by making loans and charging interest on the money they lend. They need customers for their credit products such as mortgages, car loans, personal loans, business loans, and credit cards. But if creditors make loans to people who can't pay them back, they lose money. Therefore, they need a reliable tool for evaluating their potential customers' creditworthiness before extending them a loan. After many decades of being refined, this tool has evolved into today's credit score. The credit score is not designed only by one company. In fact, there are several companies that make credit scoring software, but only one stands out above the others and is used to make more than 95% of all lending decisions in the United States—and that score is the Classic FICO®[1] credit score made by FICO® (formally named Fair Isaac Corporation until they recently changed their name to FICO®).

Because the soundness of the lenders' decisions greatly affects their bottom line, the quality of your credit score can have a significant impact on which financial opportunities are open to you and the price you will ultimately pay for them.

HOW YOUR SCORE GETS GENERATED

Interestingly, you don't have just one static credit score. You have many of them, and they are changing all the time. In fact, your score does not actually exist at any given point in time until a re-

---

[1] FICO® is a registered trademark of Fair Isaac Corporation.

quest is made for it and it is compiled by one of the companies that have been collecting and storing information about your financial interactions. The data, stored in an enormous database, has been provided to them by your creditors, and upon request is compiled into your *credit report* from the information these companies have on file, which is also the information that gets analyzed and then equated into your 3-digit credit score that tells the potential creditor the likelihood that you will have a major derogatory over the next 24 months. A major derogatory is a 90-day late payment or worse, any public record showing on your credit report, a collection, a repossession, a foreclosure, a settled account or a charge-off. The higher your score, the less the chance you will be one of those people to have a major derogatory over the next 24 months.

The credit score is a snapshot at a specific point in time of the information contained in your credit report, also called a credit history. It tells lenders your current credit status. Therefore, as new information is added to your credit report and other information gets deleted or drops off, your score fluctuates.

The companies that collect and maintain consumer credit data are referred to as consumer reporting agencies or credit reporting agencies (CRAs). They are also commonly referred to as credit bureaus. There are many consumer reporting agencies in the United States; however, there are only three major ones, commonly referred to as the Big Three. They are Equifax®, Experian®, and TransUnion™.[2]

A data furnisher, on the other hand, is any company that reports information to the credit bureaus. Among others, your creditors are data furnishers. Thus, every time you miss or are late on a payment to a creditor, that creditor has the option of reporting your delinquency to one or more of the three major credit bureaus. CRAs are in the business of gathering this information and selling it to creditors and others who are interested in how you have been handling your credit accounts.

---

[2] Equifax® is a registered trademark of Equifax Inc., Experian® is a registered service mark of Experian Information Solutions, Inc., and TransUnion™ is a registered trademark of TransUnion LLC.

HOW IT ALL COMES TOGETHER

When a lender is considering giving you a loan, they will request your credit history in the form of a credit report from one or all of the three major credit bureaus. Specifically, the credit report is a compilation of data that reflects how you have borrowed and repaid your debts, how timely you are paying your bills, and how much debt you currently have, among other things. By the time we reach adulthood, nearly every American will have a credit history with the three major credit bureaus.

Upon request, credit bureaus give their computer servers the instructions to pull together your report from the millions of bits of data in their database, based on the identifying information they have about you. The result is your credit report for that moment in time.

WHAT A CREDIT REPORT REVEALS ABOUT YOU

A credit report contains certain types of information and not others. For example, it has personal identifying information, such as your birth date, Social Security number, current and previous addresses, and present and former employers. Among the information *not* included in your credit report is your income, gender, national origin, race, or religion.

The report tells the history and status of many of your credit accounts, known as "trade lines." It lists specific details about these credit accounts, including the date the account was opened, the type of account it is (whether revolving or installment, for example), if the account is open or closed, the amount of the required monthly payment, the maximum credit limit, the most ever owed at one time in the past on the account, the latest activity on the account, its current balance, and any amounts that are currently past due. The report also includes the addresses and telephone numbers of the creditors, if you're lucky!

Each account listed also is assigned a code that reflects your payment history on the account. Are your payments current or are they 30, 60, or 90 days past due? Has the account gone so far delinquent that it has been charged off? Is there a repossession or other collection activity? The report will list accounts that have been turned over to a collection agency. In addition, a credit report will include certain public record information, such as court judgments, tax liens, and bankruptcies.

Credit reports can be somewhat challenging to read and understand. That's in part because they were originally designed as a tool for lenders, with consumers as merely an afterthought.

THE CREDIT SCORE AS A COROLLARY
TO THE CREDIT REPORT

A credit report does not automatically contain a credit score. The score must be requested separately. If a credit score is requested, the credit bureau receiving the request uses a credit scoring software program that analyzes the contents of the credit report and comes up with a score. Thus, your credit score is a corollary to your credit report.

And, as I mentioned, you don't have just one credit score. There are a couple of main reasons for this. First, the actual software program being used to analyze and calculate the score will vary between credit bureaus and lenders. It's just like other software you use at work or home, where updates and new editions come out from time to time. Credit scoring software gets updated too, changing the way it analyzes and scores certain data, thereby giving more or less weight to some items in the credit report and accordingly affecting the score. These updates will reflect changes in the industry or in society at large that affect lending practices.

For example, in the past, consumer finance accounts such as Household Finance and Beneficial Finance were given only to people with poor credit, and therefore if found on a credit report were analyzed by the credit scoring software as being more of a risk. The software thus penalized the person's score. But as times changed and these types of accounts became more popularly used in other contexts that did not equate to risk, newer models of credit scoring software were updated to not penalize the score as much when this type of account appeared on the report. (Sadly, some current scoring models still penalize you for having these types of accounts, even though they do not necessarily indicate higher risk.)

In another example, in the newest version of the leading credit scoring software, dubbed by the media as "FICO® 08," collections that are less than $100 at their initial reporting date will not hurt your score even if they later go above $100 due to interest and fees. Previous versions of the credit scoring software penalized this type of account and would result in a lowered score if you had this type of account on your report.

Each bureau integrates several kinds of credit scoring software, each with its own rules for how it reads and grades the data in the report. Depending on which credit scoring company, which model, and even the different versions within the same model of credit scoring software the bureau uses, your score can fluctuate quite a bit— sometimes in excess of 100 points!

The second main reason your credit score varies between credit bureaus is that the credit report each bureau generates on you (and thus from which they derive your score) will contain data at least slightly different from the last time it was generated, if not much more different. This is because the data collected about you by each bureau will be different and also change sometimes on a daily basis depending on when each creditor updates their information about you to the credit bureaus. This happens in part because not all companies that are reporting information about you report to all three bureaus. In fact, only about 80% of credit accounts in the U.S. get reported to all three major CRAs. Therefore, if a collection account reports to only two of the Big Three bureaus, you may have a high score and a low score that varies between the three bureaus by more than 100 points.

THE FIVE FACTORS AFFECTING YOUR SCORE

Remember, the purpose of the credit score is to help lenders predict how likely you are to pay a credit account late over the next 24 months with a major derogatory. Not long ago, very little was known about how credit scoring worked, as the developers of the credit scoring software kept it a carefully guarded secret. Fortunately, today, after much public outcry to better understand credit scoring models, we at least know the basic formula for how a score is derived. The remaining information had to be gleaned through analyzing the same person's credit reports from different times with different data being reported. The more of these "before and after" scenarios that are analyzed, the more we understand the hidden secrets the credit scoring software contains. This book will give you the benefit of my knowledge from analyzing thousands of these "before and after" scenarios.

There are five main factors considered to be the predictive indicators as to whether you will pay on time or go into serious derogatory status. Each factor is weighted differently as to how much it affects your score. These factors accumulate into the five main categories shown in the pie chart below. A lengthy discussion of each factor appears in Chapter 3.

The Factors That Determine Your Credit Score

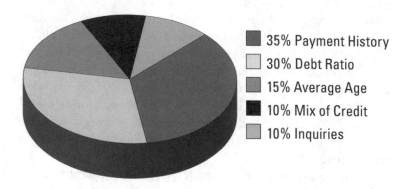

- 35% Payment History
- 30% Debt Ratio
- 15% Average Age
- 10% Mix of Credit
- 10% Inquiries

WHO CREATES CREDIT SCORES?

While there are a variety of different credit scoring models created by different companies, two are standouts in the lending industry—FICO® as of right now and possibly the VantageScore®[3] in the future.

FICO®

By far the leading industry standard—the one that most lenders use—is the scoring model created by FICO® called the "Classic FICO® model." FICO® is so much the standard, in fact, that you will often hear any credit score referred to inaccurately as a "FICO® score."

Like other software manufacturers who provide programs that you use on your home or office computer, FICO® has developed different versions and updates of their software over the years, in which their formulas for calculating scores have changed slightly and thus will affect how scores turn out.

FICO's Classic FICO® model is the standard in the mortgage industry, while FICO's industry-specific "Auto Industry Option Score" is the standard in the automotive industry. The Auto Industry Option Score is basically the Classic FICO® score with a few tweaks to make it more predictive of auto loan repayments. Many auto lenders still use the Classic FICO® rather than the Auto Industry Option Score, which is a good indication of how similar they really are. The latest credit scoring model from FICO® was dubbed "FICO® 08" by the media, but keep in mind that it is just the newest version in the Classic FICO® family. FICO® has other scoring models too, such as the "Next Generation" scoring model and, as I eluded to earlier, "Industry Option" scoring models for the automotive, mortgage, and consumer finance industries, to name a few.

For the purposes of credit repair, I suggest not worrying about any version of FICO® other than Classic FICO®, as it is the one used in more than 95% of all credit transactions.

---

[3] VantageScore® is a registered trademark of VantageScore Solutions, LLC.

VantageScore®

A fairly recent competitor to FICO® is the VantageScore®. This scoring model, developed collaboratively by Experian®, Equifax®, and TransUnion™, is making a run at FICO® in an attempt to gain market share in the extremely lucrative industry of credit scoring. While this has caused alarm among many consumer advocacy groups who are concerned that if the VantageScore® should take over, it will lead to a monopoly in the credit scoring arena (since it is owned 100% by the same people providing the credit report), the VantageScore® is not likely to take over FICO's market share just yet. It may, however, become a serious contender in doing so over the next 10 years.

Though there are some potential advantages for lenders in using the VantageScore®—for example, the data pool used to develop the VantageScore® formula has more than double the number of people than FICO's for determining what factors are predictive of serious delinquency—VantageScore® is not yet fully tested in the marketplace, and lenders are not likely to switch to a product without knowing what kind of results the model will give them in approving loans.

For this reason, it's important that before seeking a loan you obtain your true FICO® score, so that you will have a more accurate view of how lenders and others checking your credit history are seeing you.

Other credit scoring providers include the bureaus themselves with their own individual versions that they offered before creating the VantageScore® as a team effort, plus many other providers too numerous and unimportant to mention. For now, know your Classic FICO® score and keep the VantageScore® on your radar while treating all other scoring models as meaningless since almost no lender will make a decision based on their score.

WHAT'S A GOOD SCORE & WHAT DOES IT MEAN?

Both with FICO® and VantageScore®, the higher your score, the lower are the odds that you will default on a loan with a major derogatory. For Classic FICO®, the published range of the credit score is 300–850, with 850 being a perfect score. VantageScore's range is 501–990, again, with the higher score representing a lower likelihood of risk. Because FICO® is by far the scoring model leader, from here on I will be referring solely to FICO® when discussing credit scores.

So, why 300–850? A score of 850 is the unicorn, the Lock Ness Monster—no one has this perfect score; likewise, no one has a 300. It's the published range, but the reality is that most people score between 600 and 700. The lowest score I know to exist is 353. The highest is 839.

Here's how the range of scores is rated:

Excellent	760–850
Good	700–759
Fair	620–699
Poor	300–619

As discussed, the Classic FICO® credit scoring model used by the majority tells lenders how likely you are to be 90 days late or worse over the next two years on repaying a loan, be it a car loan, mortgage, or credit card.

FICO® derived this formula by analyzing consumers' habits. They went to the Big Three credit bureaus and asked for 1.5 million random credit reports from each bureau. Two years later, they asked for an update on those same consumers' credit reports. Keep in mind that the three bureaus may or may not have had the same person in their 1.5 million sample, so just because Jane Doe was one of the 1.5 million people used for Experian® does not mean she was (or wasn't) used for one or both of the other two credit bureaus. This is why the scores come out slightly different for each bureau even if all of the data used to generate the three scores is the same, because the formula was made with non-identical samples between each of the three bureau scoring models.

FICO® engineers then observed who had paid 90 days late or worse during those two years. They further analyzed those people's reports by looking at the information contained on both the original report and the updated report for that particular consumer. The goal was to figure out what other elements on the credit report those who had a major derogatory had in common and then assign score values to each element in an attempt to predict when a similarly situated consumer would also default within 24 months from the day the lender pulls the report in the future. While not an exact science, this method is actually very efficient and surprisingly accurate when studied over time.

Why these particular objectives: 90 days late or worse in 24 months? Because it's a generic enough answer that any type of lender can use it: auto lenders, credit card lenders, student loan providers, mortgage lenders, and so on. All different types of lenders are at least comfortable with what's being indicated in this benchmark. Thus, the standard of 90 days late or worse over the subsequent 24 months has not changed in 20 years.

Consumer Default: What Are the Odds?

Below is a chart from FICO's website that indicates the odds that a consumer with a particular credit score will become 90 days late or worse on a loan over the next two years.

SCORE	ODDS
800 & above	1%
750 to 799	2%
700 to 749	5%
650 to 699	14%
600 to 649	31%
550 to 599	51%
500 to 549	70%
Below 500	89%

WHAT A LOW SCORE CAN COST YOU

While it used to be that a poor credit score would get you turned down for credit, the confidence gained by the increasing reliance on credit scores has led lenders into something called "risk-based pricing." With this pricing model, if your score is low, you can still get credit, just at a much higher interest rate. Lenders feel that the higher price is justified because of your higher risk of defaulting.

Allow me to digress for a moment and inform you about a lowly practice exercised by lenders for years now, commonly known as "universal default." Even though this is not directly related to your credit score, it usually occurs when your score goes down because late payments lower your score. Many credit card companies mention this practice in the small print of their agreements, and it gives them the right to increase your interest rate if you pay 30 days late on *any* of your credit accounts, not just your account with them. Worse still, under "universal default," the interest rates shoot up to some exorbitant number, usually more than 30% APR. Thankfully, the recently enacted "Credit Card Bill of Rights" put an end to this, but some of these types of lowball tactics survived and will continue to give lenders the power to dupe consumers in certain situations. Come on, folks, you didn't honestly think that all of the lobbying money spent by the banks would allow a completely level playing field, did you?

Okay, let's get back to "risk-based pricing."

Compare 30-year fixed rates on a $500,000 home

To get a better sense about how your credit score affects interest rates on loans, see the chart below for the cost of a 30-year fixed mortgage on a $500,000 home and the rates that were being offered for each scoring range in the recent past.

FICO® SCORE	APR RATE	MONTHLY PAYMENT	INTEREST PAID
720–850	5.3%	$2,776.52	$499,549
700–719	5.9%	$2,965.68	$567,647
680–699	6.5%	$3,160.34	$637,722
620–679	7.6%	$3,530.37	$770,937
560–619	8.4%	$3,809.19	$871,305
500–599	9.9%	$4,350.95	$1,066,352

Now, in the realistic hypothetical below, see how two people with everything being equal except their credit scores would fare over time with the rates offered above in conjunction to each of their credit scores.

Jack & Brad: $500,000/30-Year Fixed

	JACK	BRAD
Salary	Equal	Equal
Credit Score	681	595
Yearly Savings	$14,288	$0
Interest Saved Over 30 Years	$428,630	$0
10% Return on Savings Compounded Total in 30 Years (Assuming the savings were invested)	$2,476,911	$0

As you can see in the above example, having a higher credit score in addition to investing the money saved as a result can lead to a multimillion-dollar payoff. A low credit score costs you big!

OTHER IMPORTANT WAYS YOUR CREDIT SCORE AFFECTS YOU

Even if you've been turned down for a loan because of a poor credit score, you may not be aware of just how far into your life this number reaches.

In recent years, credit scores have been increasingly used by important individuals and groups *other than lenders* to make decisions about doing business with you. Homeowner's insurance companies, car insurance companies, utility companies, landlords, and even employers are among those that consider your credit history and/or credit score when deciding to extend their products and services to you.

And, believe it or not, this is all perfectly legal. Insurance carriers have found that a lower credit score indicates a higher rate to insure someone, and they are legally allowed to pull your credit report to reset your premiums based on your credit. Potential employers can use your credit report as part of the screening process to make their hiring decision. Cell phone service providers use your credit score to decide whether or not to render you services or require you to place a security deposit to open an account with them. At the very worst, a poor credit profile and/or credit score can cost you your job or make it difficult to find a place to live.

Thus, your credit performance and resulting credit score can have a huge impact on many areas of your life. While a good credit score combined with other financial assets such as a strong income can help you reach your dreams—buy a house, buy a car, obtain insurance for both, get a business or student loan, or even just acquire a job or secure a place to live—a poor credit score, conversely, will deny you, or force you to pay thousands more for, those same things.

With all this being the case, you can see how imperative it is that your credit score be the best it can be. Keep reading, this book will help you achieve exactly that.

2

The "Imperfect" Credit Reporting System and the "Less Than Perfect" Credit Scoring Software Analyzing It

We've discussed the tremendous impact a credit score can have on a person's life, and many people today are feeling the repercussions of prior poor credit performance. While negative marks on a credit report may seem a fair punishment for bad financial choices, inexperience, or just plain neglect, sometimes financial setbacks are beyond our control. People do learn from their mistakes and deserve a second chance to show that they have become creditworthy. Furthermore, as you'll see, all too frequently the negative marks on a credit report are due to errors caused by information furnishers or the credit bureaus themselves. These inaccurate derogatories hurt the consumer all the same—and there's certainly nothing fair about that.

In this chapter, we'll look at the some of the flaws in the credit reporting and credit scoring systems and how this becomes unfair to consumers, including the types of errors that can occur and how the responsible parties fail to correct them. We'll also look at the tools consumers *do* have for fighting back, beginning with the Fair Credit Reporting Act.

FAIR CREDIT REPORTING ACT (FCRA)

Dealing with billions of bits of data for hundreds of millions of consumers, the credit reporting system is highly susceptible to errors. These errors, of course, can be either to the consumers' benefit or detriment, raising or lowering the credit score from where it actually "should" be. With the increasing power credit scores have over consumers' lives, it's the mistakes that impact us negatively that we're most concerned about.

As such, over the decades of credit reporting, there has been a huge public demand for truth and accuracy in credit reporting and scoring. In 1970 the outcry from the public must have outweighed the special interest money the politicians were getting from the banking lobby, because Congress responded by enacting the Fair Credit Reporting Act (FCRA) as a means of protecting consumers in their dealings with the credit bureaus. Among the FCRA protections for consumers are limitations as to who can request a consumer's credit report and how long negative information can stay on a report. The FCRA also requires credit bureaus to follow certain procedures to ensure that credit reports are as accurate as possible, even though many of these requirements are ignored by the bureaus or do not rise to the level of detail the law was meant to require.

Because errors can occur in many different ways, perhaps the most important protection provided by the FCRA is that it grants consumers the right to dispute the errors they find in their credit reports. Under the FCRA, both the credit bureaus and the party furnishing the information (creditors, lenders, collection agencies, and so forth) are required to investigate consumers' disputes and correct or eliminate data that is found to be inaccurate, unverifiable, obsolete, or incomplete.

Before we get into how the disputing process works, let's look at some of the more common errors that you are likely to find in your credit report.

ERRORS HARMING CONSUMERS

Despite the importance of accuracy in credit reporting and the protections set forth by the FCRA, errors in credit reports abound, causing great harm to consumers: 1) through the denial of credit, insurance, or employment; 2) in the granting of credit or insurance but at much higher rates; and, perhaps most detrimental of all, 3) in the tremendous time, energy, and opportunity that is lost by consumers and in the stress they incur in trying to correct inaccuracies with the credit bureaus and information providers, often with poor results.

In fact, it is estimated that serious errors or inaccuracies occur on as many as 25% of credit reports. This would mean that millions upon millions of Americans are subject to the denial of credit and other negative consequences that occur because of inaccurate information.

Though there are many types of errors that can plague a credit report, we will focus on a few of the most common and flagrant ones:

- the mixing or "merging" of multiple consumers' credit files by the credit bureaus

- the false credit history created by identity theft, including the creation of new credit accounts and negative payment history on those accounts, plus increased debt ratio overall

- inaccurate information reported to the credit bureaus by creditors, such as a debt being assigned to the wrong consumer or repayment histories being reported inaccurately

- illegal inquiries

- failure to report credit limits

- debt collection abuses, such as duplicate accounts and "re-aging" of accounts by updating the date of first delinquency with the original creditor

Mixed or Merged Files

When a credit bureau includes the credit information of one consumer in the file of another consumer, one or both consumers' credit histories report inaccurately. This occurrence is known as a "mixed" or "merged" file, and it most commonly occurs when there are similarities in identifying information between two consumers, such as in their names or Social Security numbers.

This type of error occurs in large part because of the over-inclusive criteria credit bureaus use when pulling together data to compile a credit report. For example, the credit bureaus will include account information in a consumer's file when the Social Security numbers do not match exactly but other information matches. Thus, they have been known to merge files when the consumers' names are similar and they share seven of nine digits in their Social Security numbers.

It's important to realize, too, that the credit bureaus' main goal is to please their paying customers—meaning creditors, not consumers. Thus it makes sense that they have designed the credit reporting system to include more potentially derogatory information on a consumer than less, even if all of the information cannot be matched with absolute certainty to that consumer. To the credit bureaus, this is justification enough to allow mixed files.

In most cases, only lenders benefit from this practice. Indeed, because of today's increased use by lenders of "risk-based pricing," a credit score that is lowered due to errors may even result in the lender making more profit, because the consumer will be charged a higher rate for the credit they receive.

Identity Theft

Often dubbed the "fastest growing crime" in America, identity theft adversely affects millions of consumers—and their credit scores—every year. A hybrid of the mixed file problem described above, it has become a serious source of inaccuracies in the credit reporting system.

Even though the identity thief is to blame here, part of the responsibility also falls on the shoulders of the credit bureaus and data furnishers. Their over-inclusive criteria mentioned above often allows account information to be included even when the identifiers don't perfectly match, such as when an identity thief uses the victim's last name and Social Security number, but not the first name or address.

Errors from Information Furnishers

Creditors and other data furnishers also introduce many errors into the credit reporting system. These errors usually fall into two types: 1) the inaccurate reporting of payment history, current payment status, or account balance, and 2) the attribution of a credit account to the wrong consumer.

The first type of mistake can occur easily through human error: clerks making mistakes in data entry or applying payments to the wrong account. The second type of error, where the account's "ownership" is in dispute, can occur when a spouse or other authorized user who should not be is being reported as liable for the debt. Other times, the consumer may have been the victim of identity theft.

Information being reported by a data furnisher to the credit bureaus automatically appears in consumers' credit reports. In fact, the credit bureaus are notorious for blindly accepting without any quality review the information they get from data furnishers, even if that information blatantly contradicts other information found in a consumer's credit file.

Illegal Inquiries

Did you know that it is illegal to access another's credit report without their consent? The FCRA clearly states that a consumer's credit report can be accessed only for the purposes of offering credit, insurance, housing, or employment, with the only exception being current creditors of the consumer that want to pull an updated report on the consumer to see how their credit stands. This works to ensure consumer privacy from those who would be curious about their financial status and relationships, and helps to protect against identity theft. Punishments for this "crime" include civil and criminal penalties. Yes, it's illegal to snoop into another's credit report without their permission if you are not a current creditor of theirs!

Car dealerships have been notoriously abusive in this regard. While a customer is out test-driving, a salesperson wanting to size up the customer to see if he is really worth the salesperson's time will request a credit report, all without the consumer ever knowing about it until it shows up later under the Inquiries section of their credit report.

And since inquiries do have an impact on the credit score, this abuse can have an adverse effect on the consumer's credit score.

Missing Credit Limits

You'll recall from Chapter 1 that the balance-to-credit limit ratio (primarily on revolving type accounts), also called the utilization ratio, is one of the main factors making up a credit score. Specifically, it accounts for 30% of the score. So, what then happens if a creditor fails to report a credit account's credit limit? Inevitably, the score is lowered due to a falsely calculated utilization ratio.

Here's how it works. If you have a balance of, let's say, $900 on a credit card that has a $1,000 limit, your utilization ratio would be very high (90%), which would significantly lower your score. Conversely, a balance of $100 against your $1,000 limit produces a low (10%) utilization ratio and would generally raise your score. If no credit limit is reported, then determining the true utilization ratio—of credit used to credit available—is difficult, if not impossible. In these cases, most credit scoring systems will simply take the highest reported balance in the past for that account (kept track of by Experian®, Equifax®, and TransUnion™ in a separate field in the credit report) and use that number as the account's credit limit. The smaller the percentage of the credit limit a consumer has used in the past, the more inaccurate this error would reflect in the score.

Capital One[4] was a prime culprit of this practice, having not reported credit limits for many of their consumers. They argued that limits were proprietary and that keeping limits a secret gave them a competitive advantage in the marketplace. In other words, they felt that revealing credit limits gave their

[4] Capital One is a federally registered service mark.

competitors insight into their underwriting criteria for offering credit—something they didn't want to do. Another offender of failing to report credit limits in the past was Citibank®[5].

Also interesting is that Equifax's credit reports have stood out as much more frequently missing credit limits than the other two big CRAs. This may be at least in part due to the fact that Equifax® requires creditors to fill in an extra field when reporting a credit limit.

And there's more to this story than first meets the eye. In this day and age of risk-based pricing, where credit is granted to those with poor credit but at a much higher rate, there is something particularly disturbing about the practice of creditors not reporting limits.

This leads us to the question: With lenders able to charge higher rates to consumers with lower credit scores, will the system then favor lowering scores? The answer seems obvious, and it's a scary proposition for consumers.

Debt Collection Errors and Abuses

One error that commonly occurs with accounts that have been charged off and sent to collections is that a single charged-off account often results in two or even three negative accounts on the consumer's credit report. This happens because the debt often gets reported once by the original creditor and again by the debt collector. Then, if that collector fails at collecting the debt and the account is sold to yet a third collector, another negative entry could be added to the consumer's credit report if the previous collector fails to delete their entry once they give the account to the new collection agency.

There should only be one third-party collector showing on a consumer's credit report in addition to the original creditor, but this may not always happen and you'll have to fight to get the second third-party collector to remove their entry from the credit report. The only time it is okay to have more than the original creditor and one collector reporting on the same debt is if a judgment is obtained by the collector, in which case there would be a third

---

[5] Citibank is a trademark and service mark of Citigroup Inc. and Citibank, N.A.

instance being reported in association with a single debt. The reason the third instance is okay in this case is that it is a public record, not a reported trade line like the original creditor and the collector.

A second common error is the result of a sneaky tactic on the part of collection agencies known as "re-aging." When a debt becomes charged off or sent to collections, the "date of first delinquency with the original creditor" that led to the account being charged off is a set date that should never change—even if the collection is sold several times. This is important because, as you will learn later in this book, negative credit items are supposed to remain on a credit report for only a certain length of time (for late payments, that time is 7 years). Therefore, this is the date that the bureaus use to determine when to purge the account from their database.

What normally happens with re-aging, then, is that debt collectors often use a later date as being the date of first delinquency, such as the date they acquired the debt or the date of last activity—meaning when a payment was made or a new agreement for payment was reached with the consumer—and report this as the date of first delinquency. When the date of first delinquency with the original creditor is reported inaccurately, the negative entry can remain on the credit report longer than it should, thus keeping the credit score lower for longer, as well as decreasing the score further because recent derogatories hurt the score more than older ones do.

It is thought that collection agencies continue to practice re-aging in the attempt to increase the likelihood of collecting on a debt. As you will also learn, debts are subject to a statute of limitations (SOL) as to how long after a charge-off the creditor can sue you to collect the debt. By re-aging, the SOL clock gets restarted and the collection agent has much more leverage to get you to pay—assuming, of course, that you don't call them on it and fight back.

THE DISPUTE PROCESS

As mentioned earlier in this chapter, the credit bureaus are required by the FCRA to "follow reasonable procedures to assure maximum possible accuracy" in credit reporting. Unfortunately, the credit bureaus often fail to meet their obligations in this regard. And in the processing of billions of pieces of data for hundreds of millions of files, it's understandable that sometimes things do go wrong. So to protect those consumers for whom inaccuracies do occur, the FCRA put in place a second level of protection: the dispute process. Following is a brief summary of how the dispute process is "designed" to work.

If a consumer finds an error in their credit report, they have the right to dispute the inaccurate item with the credit bureau that issued the report. To make a dispute, the consumer sends a letter to the credit bureau describing the error and providing any backup documentation that would support their claim. Upon receiving the dispute, the bureau has 30 days to complete their investigation from the time they receive the dispute (or 45 days if the report used in reference to the dispute was from *www.AnnualCreditReport.com*).

The credit bureau must conduct what the FCRA calls a "reasonable" investigation, where they review and take into consideration "all relevant information" provided by the consumer. Also, within five days of receiving the dispute, the bureau must send a notice to the information furnisher about the dispute. Again, all relevant information provided by the consumer about the dispute must be included in the notice to the information furnisher.

The furnisher, then, upon receiving notice of the dispute, must conduct its own investigation, according to the FCRA, which includes reviewing all relevant information about the dispute that has been provided by the credit bureau. After completing their investigation, they must report their results to the credit bureau. If the disputed items are found to be inaccurate, the furnisher reports this finding to the credit bureau and the credit bureau must make the correction in the consumer's credit history file.

Once they've completed their investigation, the credit bureau must send the written results to the consumer, and if the dispute has resulted in a change to the report, they must include a free copy of the new credit report.

If the credit bureau fails to complete their investigation within the 30 days, they must delete the disputed item from the credit report. If a disputed item has been deleted from the credit report, the credit bureau cannot reinsert the item back into the consumer's credit report unless they notify the consumer in writing within five days of doing so.

CRAS: DOING THEIR JOB?

The above is how the FCRA mandates the process to work. What it doesn't account for, however, is the general lack of incentive on the part of the credit bureaus and information furnishers to do a proper job that subverts these protections for the consumer. To save time and money in a process that only harms their own bottom line, the credit bureaus and information furnishers will cut corners every chance they get.

Following are the primary ways they achieve getting around the requirements of the FCRA, the result of which is effectively short-changing the consumer of a meaningful and substantive investigation of their dispute.

The credit bureaus:

1. Convert the often painstakingly written dispute letters submitted by consumers into a standardized 2- or 3-digit code summarizing the nature of the dispute. Credit bureau employees or their foreign vendors often take no more than mere seconds to match the dispute to one of 26 possible codes. This automated system is heavily dependent upon these standardized dispute codes, yet these codes are entirely inadequate in many instances to properly convey information about a dispute.

2. Fail to forward to creditors and other information providers (furnishers) the supporting documentation supplied by the consumer—documentation such as account applications, billing statements, letters, and payoff statements that can often show unquestionable proof as to the consumer's dispute. The failure to include these documents in the investigation process is itself a violation of the FCRA, and yet it is the standard practice of the CRAs.

You'll recall that the FCRA also requires information furnishers to take part in resolving disputes by conducting an investigation of their own. But, very much like the credit bureaus, furnisher investigations are usually perfunctory and meaningless, with the furnishers oftentimes doing no more "investigating" than simply comparing what is being objected to in the dispute to the information on their computer screen. In other words, they merely "verify" that the disputed information correctly reflects their own records without assuming that they may have inaccurate information about the consumer.

To add insult to injury, the credit bureaus then accept without question the furnisher's decision about the outcome of the dispute. Having done no independent review of their own, the bureaus simply repeat back the furnisher's results. And in the whole process, the consumer's complaint has never been truly investigated in a substantial or meaningful way.

When we ask ourselves why it goes this way, we need look no farther than considering who the paying customer of the credit bureau is. It's certainly not the consumer! The consumer revenue—coming from the few credit reports or other products like credit monitoring that they sell to consumers—while profitable, pales in comparison to the money generated from the banks.

And even though credit bureaus can be fined up to $1,000 per violation for selling information they know to be inaccurate after they've been notified by the consumer, this has proven to be an insufficient incentive for them to change their practices. The credit bureaus are only too aware of who pays their bills; it's the lender or other information furnisher who uses or supplies the data in the credit bureaus' massive databases. Credit bureaus make money by selling data, not by handling disputes and correcting credit reports. These obligations mandated by the FCRA only detract from their profit margin.

And despite the tremendous importance of the dispute process to millions of individual American lives as well as the national economy, the FCRA has done little to enforce its regulations and make the CRAs and information furnishers fall in line.

CRAS: MAKING MONEY OFF OF YOU

Most people don't realize that the credit bureaus make the big money by marketing you and your behavior to the highest bidder. Here are a few of the ways the CRAs are raking in hundreds of millions by selling your data:

- Helping lenders scout you with targeted marketing leads. This results in the pre-approved credit card offers you get in the mail.

- Selling your current info to debt collectors. The bureaus sell your information to any collector that is trying to collect money from you. These collectors are considered to have a "permissible purpose" since the debt they are collecting originated with a creditor that had the right to pull your report.

- Alerting collectors to mortgage/car loan inquiries. Since mortgage inquiries usually mean a mortgage application with tons of strings attached, collectors love to know when you are trying to get a mortgage so they can do everything in their power to prevent that from going through—unless you pay them off, of course!

- Alerting your creditors when a late payment shows up so the creditors that apply "universal default" can start collecting their inflated interest rate right away.

FIGHTING BACK WITH CREDIT REPAIR

Considering the numerous errors on credit reports that can and do occur, consumers often find the credit reporting system itself stacked against them. And given that less-than-perfect credit causes severe repercussions to the consumer, you can see why consumers could use a little extra muscle on their side of this tug of war.

What Credit Repair Can Do for You

At its most basic, credit repair is simply a process of paying off debt obligations and letting any negative marks that they caused expire from your credit history while creating new positive credit that will replace them.

More aggressive credit repair means removing inaccurate, misleading, or unverifiable marks (in other words, "questionable" negative credit) from your credit report, thereby increasing your score. And since it is rare that an item is reported 100% accurately, virtually every credit problem imaginable—from charge-offs to tax liens—can be challenged and oftentimes removed.

The Ethics of Credit Repair

There has been some question as to the ethics of credit repair, particularly disputing accurate information on the credit report as inaccurate. The bottom line is that the credit repair expert is fighting for the consumer in a broken system by giving it a taste of its own medicine. Because there are so many ways that the credit score is unfair to the consumer, if anything, credit repair merely helps to even out the scale.

Still not convinced? In addition to the abuses and errors mentioned in this chapter, here are a few other ways the credit score is unfair to the consumer in how it relates to the structure of credit reporting:

1. Every month, most of your creditors report to the credit bureaus regarding the status of your account along with the balance and other such information. A majority of creditors report your balance when your statement closes for the month—on your statement closing date, not your payment due date—which means that even if you pay your balance in full every month you still have a balance being reported for the entire 30 days of that month. This, of course, lowers your credit score due to an artificially high debt ratio. It's intentionally set up that way to prejudice the consumer in the creditor's favor. (A way to avoid this, by the way, is to call

your credit card company and find out when they report to the bureaus and send them a payment early enough to assure that the payment posts before they report. This also has the side benefit of you having a low balance for the next 30 days even if you have a maxed-out credit card on Day 2 of the 3-day statement cycle in between reporting periods.)

2. You pay a collection or a charge-off and your credit score goes down. Even though it is illegal to re-age a collection account when either it is paid in full, a partial payment is made, or the account is sold to another collection agency, collection agencies violate this all of the time and, as a result, leave you with a lower score.

With credit repair, we're using the law to help the consumer. We're trying to make sure that the CRAs have good records, as they are required to do. And because the CRAs are not truly doing an investigation as the FCRA requires them to do, turnabout is only fair play! Credit repair companies use the law to get an item removed for being inaccurate or incomplete, even if they don't use the real reason the item is inaccurate. Through much trial and error, credit repair specialists have learned what dispute reasons get the best results in getting any particular item removed, and they will use that knowledge to help their clients. Yes, it's true, the credit repair process sometimes requires a little bit of cat and mouse to succeed!

The way I look at it, credit repair offers people a second chance based on a system that holds everybody down. And, usually, the people who are trying to clean their act up realize how important their credit score is and they want a second chance. If the laws that we're using to help someone out are the laws that ensure credit items get reported accurately, then how is it wrong to make sure these companies report accurately? If they can't prove that something is accurate, then the law says they have to delete that item from the credit report. In my credit repair business, I'm making sure the CRAs are doing their job according to what the law says they have to do.

In a system stacked against the middle-class-and-under consumer, where credit card companies have the intent to injure people for profit, credit repair has evolved as a vital and necessary tool to work the dispute process in the consumer's favor when requesting the correction or deletion of negative items on the credit report that are shown to have inaccuracies. It has given many a consumer a needed second chance after falling prey to any one of the many different circumstances that lead to less-than-perfect credit.

The first step to successful credit repair is seeing exactly what's on your credit report and finding out your score. We'll learn how to do that in the next chapter.

3

What's *Your* Score?

Lenders will often use your "mid score"—the middle of the three scores generated by the Big Three credit bureaus—to make their credit decisions. Therefore, it's wise to know where you stand *before* you seek new credit, as getting denied will harm your score further. Whether you want to apply for credit or you've already been turned down and want to start improving your score, the first step is to learn what information is on your credit reports and what your score is.

Following are the steps to get you started.

STEP 1: OBTAINING YOUR CREDIT REPORTS

Under a 2003 amendment to the FCRA called the Fair and Accurate Credit Transactions Act (FACT Act), Equifax®, Experian®, and TransUnion™ must each must provide you with one free credit report every 12 months if you request it. You can access this free report immediately online at *www.AnnualCreditReport.com*.

Remember, though, that this service is being provided by the credit bureaus, who are not at all pleased about having to give away their valuable information for free, nor do they want to arm you, the consumer, with tools to improve your credit. As a result of this, you will find that you have to get through a gauntlet of questions, ads, and web pages in order to successfully download your reports. If they can't make you pay with money, they'll at least try to deter you through the cost of the time it takes you to download the free reports. In many cases you will get an error that says your order cannot be completed online and that you need to call them to proceed. (I've received that error before from TransUnion™ telling me that for "security purposes" they can't give me access to my report online. Yet, miraculously, two minutes later they were able to give me my report when I purchased their zendough™[6] credit product. Must have been one of those convenient coincidences!)

In addition to requesting it online, your free credit report from *www.AnnualCreditReport.com* can also be obtained by telephone or regular mail.

To request your credit report by phone:

- Call 1-877-322-8228 and complete their verification process to get your report.
- Your reports will be mailed to you within 15 days.

To request your credit report by mail:

1. Download the request form located at *https://www.AnnualCreditReport.com/cra/order?mail.*
2. Complete the form and mail it to the address provided on the form along with any other information they request.

Note: As we will discuss in a moment, your free credit report does not include your credit score. Your credit score must be purchased separately. You can request to purchase your credit score when you request your free annual credit report, but only Equifax® offers your actual FICO® score during this ordering process at *www.Annual CreditReport.com.*

---

[6] zendough™ is a trademark of TransUnion Interactive, Inc.

STEP 2: OBTAINING YOUR CREDIT SCORES

Having access to knowledge about credit scoring is a pretty recent event. Before 2002, consumers couldn't even get their own FICO® score. Credit scores were a safely guarded secret and the only way to get them was through a lender who ran your credit report and score. Only after tremendous outcry over consumer rights for transparency in credit scoring have credit scores become available for purchase by consumers.

It's also important to know that, as mentioned above, the free service from the credit bureaus at *www.AnnualCreditReport.com* only gives you your credit reports for free, not your credit scores. At that website, you will have to pay for your credit score, and more importantly, the score you receive will *not* be a true FICO® score except for from Equifax®, which offers the FICO® score for sale during the registration process. If you recall from our earlier discussions, it's important to know your true FICO® score because that is the score lenders and others will use when evaluating granting you credit, insurance, housing, or employment. Therefore, I suggest only going to *www.AnnualCreditReport.com* if all you want is your credit reports.

The three credit bureaus do, however, offer your true FICO® scores for purchase. At the time of this writing, the place to do this for two of the three CRAs—Equifax® and TransUnion™—is *www. CreditMoves.com/fico*, which will then direct you to FICO's consumer site called "myFICO®[7]."

On Valentine's Day 2009, to show their love for FICO®, Experian® terminated their agreement to offer FICO® scores to consumers. Experian® does still sell FICO® scores to lenders, just not directly to consumers on the myFICO® website. This is a sad turn of events because, as we've discussed, with the nature of risk-based pricing and the economic downturn, consumers don't need less access to their information now, they need more access.

You will still pay more at the myFICO® consumer site for two scores than you will pay for all three at the alternative site I often recommend to clients: *www.CreditMoves.com/score*. At the time of this

---

[7] myFICO® is a registered trademark of Fair Isaac Corporation.

writing, *www.CreditMoves.com/score* offers a link to a provider that provides all three credit reports and true FICO® scores for each of the Big Three bureaus for only $20. Getting your reports and scores here will be a hard inquiry (we'll discuss this a little later), which means that it will hurt your credit score by a few points, but it is an easy way to know where you stand without having to jump through too many hoops—and the score drop is not going to be too much.

If you'd also like to check out your VantageScore®, you can order it through TransUnion™ or Experian® by going to *www.CreditMoves. com/vscore*, where direct links to each bureau are available for ordering your VantageScore®. Please note that only Experian® currently offers the VantageScore® directly to consumers, while TransUnion™ requires you to buy their new credit monitoring product zendough™ to obtain your TransUnion™ VantageScore®. And, even though there is a VantageScore® for Equifax®, as of this writing there is not a way for the consumer to order it directly. I recommend checking *www. CreditMoves.com/vscore* regularly for any updates in information regarding the Equifax® VantageScore®, to see if it has become available after the time of the printing of this book.

Though all of the bureaus use the same algorithm for determining the final VantageScore®, the data they use may have small discrepancies and therefore your VantageScore® could vary slightly between the agencies.

Minimum Criteria Needed to Generate a Credit Score

Now, getting back to the FICO® score. Note that not every credit history automatically qualifies for a credit score—it has to meet certain minimum standards to be score-able. Failure to meet the guidelines below on a particular bureau will cause that bureau's credit score to not generate and you'll see a zero in place of the score or the report will state that the minimum scoring criteria has not been met.

A credit score of zero can happen in one of three ways:[8]

---

[8] Additionally, in older versions of FICO, a credit report that had more than 100 trade lines (even if they were all positive) could also cause a zero to show in the score column because it was more data than the credit scoring model could handle, which in turn rendered the report un-scoreable.

1. The Social Security number is reported as deceased to the credit bureau.

2. There hasn't been an account open for at least six months.

3. No trade line has been updated in the past six months.

The good news is that if you get a score of zero, there are a couple of things you can do to fix the situation and begin to generate a score:

1. Open up a brand-new credit card to get rid of the zero. Within six months of opening the credit card, you'll satisfy one of the factors because an account will have been updated within the last six months. Now, the problem with this is that you still have a score of zero because you won't have an account that was opened for at least six months that was updated in the last six months until that account is six months old. At the 6-month mark, your score will begin to generate.

   You may be able to get around this sooner by getting added to someone's credit card as an authorized user (AU). The newer credit scoring models, however, are on to the AU trick and may not score the new account at all, but if they do, it will allow you to get the history of the primary cardholder and, as long as that account is older than six months, you'll get a score the second it is reported. As the newer scoring models become more popularly used, this tactic is going to become less and less effective as time goes on and therefore it is ultimately best to build your own credit.

   It's also important to be aware that when you get added to a family or friend's trade lines (credit accounts) as an authorized user, any damage on the owner's account will show on your (the AU's) account unless the owner calls and has you removed as an AU before the damage occurs. If the account is closed (like in bankruptcy), it is much harder to get them off the AU's credit report, though it is still possible. The bankruptcy (BK) of the owner is listed in the AU's account, even though the wording on the account has to say that it's another person's BK. Also with AU accounts, the AU is not responsible (not contractually liable) to pay the account, but sometimes a spouse can be held responsible because it is considered "marital debt." The only time a positive credit account can harm an AU is if the account is so new and the AU has a very long established credit history and no late payments—but then if this were the case, a person wouldn't need to be added as an AU anyway!

2. Use one of your credit cards you haven't used for a while and wait for the information to update to the credit bureau. This will satisfy the requirement that an account has been updated at least once in the past six months.

STEP 3: READING YOUR CREDIT REPORTS

Once you've obtained your credit reports, you'll want to keep an eye out for two primary concerns as you start to assess the information they contain:

1. What negative/derogatory items are in the report?

2. How much debt do you have and are the balances and limits on that debt reporting correctly?

Keep in mind that sometimes you luck out and find a mistake that is in your favor, such as having a balance reporting lower or a limit reporting higher than what it actually is. If either of these occurs, feel of good fortune—the error is helping your score by giving you a lower ratio of debt to available credit. You wouldn't complain to the car wash guy if they waxed your car when you purchased the basic car wash, would you? Same goes here.

Reason Codes: Your Credit Problems at a Glance

If your FICO® score is less than 850—and everyone's is—you can quickly identify your biggest problems by simply glancing at the "reason codes" on your report. The reason codes—listed just below your score on a "tri-merge" credit report that gives you all three scores (usually a report from a lender or a report from *www.Cred itMoves.com/score*)—tell you the general issues that have kept you from achieving a perfect score. Every credit report, even one with a score of 849, will have at least one reason code listed. This is a great convenience for getting a quick summary of the shape of your credit history before analyzing the whole report.

In the reason codes section, the primary reason you did not achieve a perfect 850 is listed first, with the remaining reasons following, ranked from top to bottom in the order of importance and effect on your score. Listed below are only a few of the more than 100 possible reason codes that could appear on a credit report:

- Account payment history is too new to rate
- Amount of credit available on revolving accounts
- Amount owed on delinquent accounts
- Amount past due on account
- Delinquency on account
- Serious delinquency
- Level of delinquency on accounts
- Lack of recently established credit accounts
- Length of time accounts have been established

Reason codes are very helpful, allowing you to assess at a glance whether paying down your debt or deleting negative items will likely increase your score.

Note that the Fair and Accurate Credit Transactions Act (FACT Act) requires credit bureaus to list as a fifth reason code (if it doesn't come in as numbers 1-4) whenever inquiries were a contributing factor of more than a couple of points for the score not being higher. You'll see "Number of Inquiries Adversely Affected the Score" given as a reason if that is a problem affecting your score.

STEP 4: UNDERSTANDING THE FIVE MAIN FACTORS THAT DETERMINE YOUR SCORE

A lot of homeowners have the mindset that making payments on time automatically equates to good credit and high credit scores. Unfortunately, this couldn't be further from the truth. While paying your bills on time accounts for a large portion of your credit score, there's still a lot more to it. In fact, paying your bills on time only drives a third of the points in your credit score, which means that two-thirds of your score has nothing to do with making on-time payments.

As mentioned in Chapter 1, five main factors go into calculating your overall credit score. It's important to understand them, as that gives you the power to make the changes necessary to increase your score. Let's briefly review each category and how much they count toward your score:

1. Payment History (past delinquencies mostly) – 35%

2. Debt-to-Credit Limit Ratio (revolving debt ratio) – 30%

3. Average Age of Credit File – 15%

4. Mix of Credit – 10%

5. Inquiries – 10%

1. Payment History: 35% of Score

Payment history, the most important category, is rather self-explanatory. You don't have to be a genius to figure out that if you pay your bills on time, you'll do well here. Likewise, if you have a history of late payments, collections, charge-offs, judgments, and other public records showing a failure to pay, you're not going to do so well. It's okay to get sued as long as it doesn't result in a judgment against you personally. If you do happen to get a judgment against you, your score will suffer more on top of the damage caused by the item that was most likely reporting as a collection or a charge-off on the report before the creditor sued you to get the judgment.

In addition to the type of negative item you have, the number of negative items on your credit report also has an impact on your score. The more incidents of credit transgression, the more your score will suffer.

Also a factor is how recent the negative information is. Recent blemishes will punish your score more than if they are several years old. The first two years from the time the negative mark occurs has the most impact on the score, but even older derogatory items hurt the score to some degree.

To avoid problems in this category, make sure to pay every single bill you have before the due date. Even if you aren't 30 days late, depending on when the creditor reports to the credit agencies, you may be reported to the CRAs as having a past due amount. For example, if your mortgage payment is due on the 15th and the lender reports on the 16th but you don't pay until the 26th, the account will be reported with a past due amount and it will hurt your score.

Although most lenders wait until you are at the 30-day late mark to report a 30-day late payment on your credit report, some will report the 30-day late when you are just *one* day late because "30 days late" on the credit report actually means 1-30 days late. At a minimum, you are past due when you pay even one day late with the difference being that a "past due" notation will disappear from your report once you become current, while a "30-day late" notation will stay for 7 years (unless you get it off sooner through the dispute process or by getting the creditor to remove it from the bureau themselves).

Each late payment or past due notation harms your score up to 100 points or more depending on the severity of the late and also depending on what else your report contains. It is impossible to give an exact point value deduction since so many factors go into your unique credit report. To tell you that a 30-day late costs you, say, 65 points is not only untrue but also devoid from logic since someone with a credit score already under 500 will seldom see any reported item cause the score to drop more than 20 points, while someone with an 810 credit score may see even a 30-day late payment cause the score to plunge 100 points.

To interpret the derogatory information in your credit reports, you can follow these general rules:

- Any information in the Public Records section of your credit report is considered a major derogatory, no exceptions.

- Any information that is equal to or worse than a 90-day late payment is also considered a major derogatory. This includes foreclosures, collections, settlements, and repossessions.

- If any of the above information is less than 24 months old, then it's going to have even more of a negative impact on your credit rating than it would if it is older than 24 months.

- If you see numerous of the above items, you're being penalized for the volume aspect as well.

Tips for this category:

✓ Timing of the delinquency: The further in the past the delinquency is, the less effect it has on the score. Time heals here.

✓ Level of delinquency: A 60-day late is worse than 30, 90 is worse than 60, and bankruptcy is the worst of all due to the cumulative effect a bankruptcy has on many accounts when those accounts update as "included in bankruptcy," also a major derogatory.

✓ Date of first delinquency: This is sometimes grouped together with the "date of last activity" even though for clarity reasons it shouldn't be. As noted, the "date of first delinquency" is the date when the first default occurred that led to the charge-off or collection. This is usually the first 30-day late payment that led to the charge-off on a credit card account or 30 days after an invoice is sent on a medical bill unless the invoice specifically gave a longer time period to pay, in which case it would be the date that time period expired. Many credit reports will not have a column for the date of first delinquency and will only have a column for the date of last activity. If you're lucky, the date of first delinquency will be mentioned in the notes; otherwise, you'll have to assume that the date of last activity is the date of first delinquency unless you are willing to go through the hassle of calling the bureaus for clarification.

✓ Past due notices: These destroy scores. If the account showing a past due amount is not in collection or charge-off status, it is best that you pay that past due amount immediately to bring the account current. If the account showing a past due balance is also a collection or a charge-off, paying the past due amount will not yield much of a credit score increase (if any at all) because the collection or charge-off status is the main factor hurting that account. Keep in mind, though, that not paying a collection account may lead to them filing a lawsuit against you, so paying these accounts is still a good idea if the amount is over $1,000. (Amounts less than $1,000 are usually not pursued in court due to the low dollar figure.) In addition to the $1,000 rule, I also suggest taking into account the statute of limitations (SOL) for your particular state to determine if the creditor's ability to sue you has expired. You'll want to do this before you agree to pay a collection or decide how much you are willing to pay. We'll discuss this at length in Chapter 4.

✓ Missing (skipping) payments (low vs. high): If you need to miss a payment, it is better to miss your $300 car payment than your $1,500 mortgage payment because the score will penalize you slightly more if the balance of your overall debt is higher than if it is lower when determining how many points will be deducted for paying late on that particular account. This is almost a non-factor and may only hurt by an extra point or so, but it is worth mentioning. The reason for this is that the credit scoring software manufacturers have noticed that usually people who miss their big payments miss them because they don't have the money, and a higher percentage of people who miss higher payments will go 90 days or more late more often than people who miss lower payments. Again, this is not a huge difference but the statistics have shown a predictive correlation in this sub-area.

✓ Collections: Pay off collections the day of the home loan closing date if the lender requires that you do so, but *not* before the loan's closing date due to the risk of the collection agency possibly re-aging the account and resetting the date of first delinquency when they update the account as paid. Though this does not happen that often, it does occur from time to time. What you don't want to happen is for you to pay the collection and then the collector re-ages the account a week before the loan closing and then the lender pulls an updated report the day before the loan closing and the score comes in below the requirement and you don't get the loan as a result of the collector's mistake. Better to be safe than sorry.

2. Revolving Debt Ratio: 30% of Score

The most important non-payment category in your credit score is, by far, the amount of debt you carry. And while your installment debt (auto loans and mortgages) are factored into your score here too, it's really your revolving debt (credit cards, for the most part) that's most important in this area. This includes anything from Visa®, MasterCard®, Discover®, American Express®, gas cards, and/or retail credit cards.[9] The balances that you carry on your credit cards in relation to the total revolving credit you have available can affect your score almost as much as whether you make your payments on time.

This category calculates the proportion of balances to credit limits on your revolving credit card accounts—also referred to as "revolving utilization." Simply put, the higher your revolving utilization percentage, the lower your score.

---

[9] Visa® is a registered trademark of Visa, MasterCard® is a registered trademark of MasterCard Worldwide, Discover® Card is a registered trademark of Discover Financial Services, Inc., and American Express® is a trademark and service mark of American Express Company, its subsidiaries and affiliates.

So, what is revolving utilization and how is it calculated? To determine your revolving utilization, you'll need to add up all of your current balances and all of your current credit limits on your open revolving credit accounts (except for Home Equity Lines of Credit). This will give you a total balance and a total credit limit. Divide the total balances by the total credit limit and then multiply that number by 100. This will give you your total revolving utilization percentage.

For example:

Total Balances		Total Limits		Total Revolving		Utilization%
$12,000	÷	$25,000	=	0.48	×100	48%

Remember, the lower your utilization percentage, the more points you'll earn and the higher your credit score will be. To earn the most possible points in this category, you should try to keep your revolving utilization at 10% or less. If you can't reach 10%, just remember that the lower the percentage, the better. While 50% is better than 60%, 40% is better than 50%, and so on.

How you pay your bills and your revolving utilization are by far the most important factors used to determine your credit score. They account for two-thirds of the points in your score. That's a hefty chunk! Needless to say, if you don't do well in both of these categories, your score isn't going to be very good regardless of how you do in the remaining areas.

While the remaining categories are worth fewer points, they are still very important if you want to earn the highest possible score, certainly a requirement in today's difficult credit environment.

To give my final thoughts on revolving debt ratio, I wanted to pose a question I frequently hear, "Is there such a thing as too much credit?" ANSWER: No! If you have a lot of *unused* credit, lenders may be shy in giving you more, but it does not hurt your credit score. That is a myth. In fact, you will have a much lower debt ratio for the debt you carry, and any big purchases you make will not destroy your score by dramatically increasing your debt ratio.

Tips for this category:

✓ Credit Cards:

➤ Pay your cards down as much as you can. The closer to zero you are, the better when it comes to revolving credit utilization.

➤ Use each credit card at least every three months to lessen the likelihood that the bank will close your card due to non-activity. Banks tend to close accounts that are not generating revenue for them, which is why you need to use it or lose it.

➤ Do not close credit cards because doing so instantly increases your revolving debt ratio.

➤ If you pay off your credit card each month, do so before the closing date so that the credit report will reflect a balance of zero all month rather than the balance the card had at the closing date.

I once did an interesting experiment with a friend who had $100,000 in credit card debt. With Power of Attorney from him, I called his credit card companies and I asked each bank he had a card with to tell me when the card's statement closing date was. Without paying down the balances even a penny overall, I simply moved money around by doing balance transfers with the balance transfer checks from each bank, strategically timing the payments on each card to assure that the balance on each card was paid off in full before the statement closing date. So, I used a balance transfer check from Chase®[10] to pay Citibank®, for example, on the 16th of the month, while turning around and using a Citibank® balance transfer check to pay off Discover®, which had a statement closing date on the 20th, and so

---

[10] Chase® is a registered trademark of JPMorgan Chase & Co.

on. Within two weeks, I had my friend's credit report showing that he had zero credit card debt even though he still owed $100,000! I could have kept it going but stopped, and it took more than three weeks for his credit report to once again show that he owed the $100,000. My friend's credit score went up over 100 points while I had his balances showing as zero on the report. Knowing how creditors report is crucial when managing your credit score.

➤ If you don't have any credit, get added as an authorized user (AU). Even though FICO® made adjustments in their latest software "FICO® 08" to bypass what they consider non-legitimate authorized user accounts, many lenders do not adopt the newest versions of the scoring model until years after its release. Given that no lenders used FICO® 08 until 2009, there are still quite a few years left that this benefit could help.

Keep in mind, though, that lenders too have caught on to this loophole and some will not approve a loan if the credit report contains accounts where the person is an authorized user. For that reason, I suggest only getting added as an authorized user if you are just starting to build credit or if you currently can't get approved and have nothing to lose by getting added as an authorized user. But remember, only get added to low-balance/high-limit credit cards with a person who pays it on time because if the primary cardholder is maxed, you're maxed; if they pay late, you paid late as far as the score is concerned.

✓ Credit Limit:

➤ Ask for credit limit increases every six months to assure you have the highest limit available in order to avoid having a high debt ratio every time you make a purchase. Say, for example, you buy a couch for $1,000 and only have one credit card with a $2,000 limit. Assuming you were at a zero balance before the purchase, you are now at 50% of your total revolving debt utilization. If, however, you had asked for several credit limit increases in the two years prior to the purchase and had a $10,000 credit limit, that $1,000 couch would leave you at only 10% utilization.

➤ Make sure the limit is reported. If a credit limit is not reported, the credit scoring software will look at the high credit on the account and assume that the high credit owed in the highest prior month is the credit limit and will score the account accordingly. The problem is that if you have a $10,000 credit limit and it is not reporting, and the most you ever spent on that credit card was $1,500, the credit scoring software will treat it as though you have a $1,500 limit. In the previous couch example, you would be at 66% utilization if the limit was not reported and the highest amount you ever owed— "the high credit"—was $1,500.

Another trick to help you in this area if you are having a hard time getting the limit reported is to simply max out the credit card and then pay it off when the bill comes. This will effectively make your high credit the same amount as your actual credit limit. American Express® cards that are not revolving cards are treated similarly to revolving credit cards with no limit reporting. Since some American Express® cards are not revolving and do not have a preset spending limit, the credit limit is left blank but the high credit is still reported, which is the number the credit score uses to score the account.

These type of non-revolving American Express® accounts are treated the same as regular revolving accounts as far as how the score weights the accounts, the only difference being that the high credit will always be treated as the limit, where a revolving credit account only uses the high credit number when the limit is missing. If both the credit limit and the high credit are missing on the credit report, the credit score will ignore the account altogether except for the payment history.

✓ Spouse:

➤ Keep your credit separate from your spouse's. The worst thing you can do is get joint credit cards with someone. Joint credit cards, unlike authorized user cards, means that both people are on the hook for the debt and also the payment history. It is also very difficult, if not impossible, to remove someone from a joint credit card account unless the account is paid to zero first. The bank has no incentive to let one person off the hook when they are owed money and won't do so unless the card is paid to zero. Even then, the bank will usually make you close the account and have both cardholders reapply for a new one if they want to separate the account. That means that both parties potentially lose an aged, seasoned account. You are better off starting without a joint account holder than to suffer down the road if you decide you want to become untied from that person.

Another reason to not get a joint account on a credit card is because the banks will usually not approve the card unless they feel comfortable with both parties; adding another applicant will usually not increase the chances of approval.

➤ Transfer debt from one spouse to another. Whenever your credit cards are separate from your spouse's, you can use each other's credit status to help each other when applying for loans as individuals. The reason this works and also another argument for why having joint credit cards is a bad idea is that one spouse can max out their credit cards to pay off the other spouse's credit cards and leave the other spouse with a much higher credit score as a result of their reduced debt utilization. Now, of course, the spouse maxing out their credit is going to see their score tank, but if the spouse with the now good credit score is applying for the loan on their own, who cares? This technique was great for getting score-driven mortgages that did not require income verification. Of course, those days are gone but there are numerous other instances where this comes in handy, like buying a car.

➤ Apply for business credit cards! The credit score only scores what it sees on the credit report. Given that most business credit cards don't report to the credit bureaus unless you default, even when you sign as a guarantor, having a few business credit cards is mandatory in protecting your credit profile. If you need to max out your business credit cards, unlike personal cards it won't hurt your credit score unless it is reporting on your personal credit report.

Most people don't realize that as long as you have a business of any kind, getting a business credit card is the same challenge as getting a personal one, which means there is no reason to not apply for a few. You will have to sign as a personal guarantor for the card unless you have a big corporation with established credit—but who cares, you're not planning on defaulting, you just want the benefit of the card not hurting your credit score in the event you need to spend significant amounts on the card. But remember, if you default, most banks will then report the account on your personal credit report, and the credit score does not treat a reported business credit card any differently than a personal one. They both get scored as revolving credit cards when they show on the report. Make sure to ask the credit card company you are planning on applying to if they report the business credit card to your personal credit report. Most won't, but some do, so be sure to inquire before you apply.

3. Average Age of Credit File: 15% of Score

Don't confuse this with *your* age! It's the age of your credit file. The score is looking to see if you have a lengthy history of managing your credit obligations. FICO® found that if someone has a long credit history, on average they don't tend to pay 90 days late or more as much as those with a short credit history.

The average age of your credit history is determined by a couple of factors related to age, namely 1) the "date opened" on the oldest account listed on your credit report and 2) the average age of all of your credit accounts in addition to when your most recent account was opened. Together these factors make up 15% of the entire credit score. The older your credit history is on average, the more points you will earn in this category. Therefore, you want your file to be as old as possible.

There's really not much you can do in this category except wait it out. As your accounts get older, you will gradually earn more points. This means that you should never try to get older, good accounts removed from your credit reports. You want the history!

The one way around this traditionally has been to get added as an authorized user (AU) on another person's old, good account. But, as we've discussed, lenders are on to this piggybacking and often won't allow reports that show an authorized user account. And, as mentioned several times, the newest version of the FICO® scoring model, FICO® 08, is reportedly not scoring accounts where this type of piggybacking is going on. Other versions of the software will, though, so it may be worth a try until all the banks are systematically using FICO® 08.

Tips for this category:

✓ The longer your credit history, the better.

✓ Hold on to old credit cards.

✓ Don't close the credit cards you have.

✓ At least every few months, use the credit cards you have. This will deter the banks from closing the accounts for inactivity to cut their risk of default or to sever ties with non-income producing cardholders, which over time would lead to a younger credit file once the closed account drops off your report. (Closed positive accounts usually fall off the report after 10 years. Open positive accounts stay forever.)

4. Mix of Credit: 10% of Score

What kind of credit accounts do you have? Does your credit report show a nice variety of different types of accounts—revolving loans and installment loans? Examples of installment credit accounts are auto loans, personal loans, mortgages, and student loans. Examples of revolving credit accounts are credit cards, home equity lines of credit (HELOCs), and retail cards. Examples of "open" credit accounts are utilities, some American Express® cards, and cell phones.

If your credit report is dominated by one type of account (or lack of others), this could negatively affect the number of points you earn in this category, the reason being that FICO® likes to see that you have a few different types of accounts. I recommend one mortgage, one auto loan, and three to five revolving credit cards as a near-perfect blend.

But because this category is only a very small percentage of your score, don't worry if you don't have this exact mix. If you have more than five credit cards, it doesn't mean that you should close some of your accounts, as having "too many" credit cards will not hurt you that much (maybe 10 points), while the effect of closing several cards could destroy your score due to debt ratio impact and, over time, a younger credit file. Any credit card debt you have will be small compared to the total limit you have, so it will benefit your score in that way; you'll benefit more than you'll be hurt by keeping credit card accounts open. If you close accounts, you may end up hurting your score if your utilization is then too high. Therefore, even if you have "Too many accounts" as one of the notations on the credit report reasons, don't do anything—certainly do not close an account, but don't open any more accounts either if you already have 10 or more credit cards.

If you don't have a mortgage and get one tomorrow, your score may increase 10 points once the account is updated as "paid as agreed" on the credit report because you will be improving upon the "healthy mix" category. A second mortgage won't change the score much, but a third mortgage will hurt the score in this area since you are starting to divert from the healthy mix by having too much of one type of credit account.

Tips for this category:

✓ A mixture is best.

✓ One mortgage account is ideal.

✓ One auto loan is ideal.

✓ Three to five revolving credit cards is optimal, but having more than five has other greater benefits that make it worth losing a few points in this category.

5. Inquiries: 10% of Score

When you apply for credit, you are giving the lender permission to pull your credit report and credit score. Each time this happens, your credit report will reflect what's called an "inquiry." To perform well in the inquiries category, you should really only apply for credit when you need it.

There are two types of inquiries—hard and soft. A "hard" inquiry occurs when you are trying to get more credit than you currently have, and this type has a negative impact on your credit score. A "soft" inquiry occurs when you ask for a copy of your own credit report or when a creditor or other party looks at your credit for a reason other than to grant credit, such as a creditor account review, new lender promotion, insurance or utilities other than a cell phone provider, or employment-related inquiries.

Mortgage- and Auto-Related Inquiries Are Treated Differently

If you are shopping for a mortgage or a car loan, it is expected that you may apply at more than one lender in order to find the best deal. Therefore, though it used to be that you could accumulate unlimited inquiries over 14 days in each of these two categories of loans (auto and mortgage are treated as two separate categories), it's now 45 days per category.

What this means is that during this 45-day window, which starts for each category once the first inquiry is pulled in that category, all auto and mortgage inquiries that are made with that 45-day window will be treated as one inquiry within each loan category. The 45-day clock starts to tick with the first inquiry made in each loan category beginning 12 months prior to the date the report and score were pulled. In order to effectively and accurately know how many inquiries you are truly being scored on, you would need to jump forward after the first 45-day window expires to the date where you see the next auto or mortgage inquiry and then start a new 45-day window and group those together until you reach the current date.

Keep in mind that credit card inquiries or non-auto/mortgage installment inquiries are scored for every individual inquiry and never grouped as one inquiry like the auto and mortgage related ones. That means that if you apply for 10 credit cards in one day, you will be scored as though you had 10 inquiries and you will see a dramatic score drop compared to 10 mortgage inquiries made on

the same day. In addition to being grouped together, auto and mortgage related inquiries will not hit and be scored until 30 days after
the first auto or mortgage inquiry was made within that particular
45-day time frame.

Inquiries can cost anywhere from 0 on the low end to 50 points
on the high end per single inquiry, but most inquiries will hurt the
score an average of 5 points per inquiry. Thus, in this example, unlimited auto and mortgage inquiries made within each 45-day window are scored as one inquiry in each category and would cost 5
points for each category (assuming that 5 points is what an inquiry
will hurt a particular borrower).

Although FICO® won't state the exact number, after you accumulate a certain number of inquiries within 12 months, you will
not be penalized for additional inquiries. My understanding from
FICO® insiders is that additional inquiries above 10 in 12 months
will not hurt the score any more. If only the first 10 inquiries will
hurt you, assuming this number is accurate, then you can have a
million inquiries in a 12-month period and it won't hurt you any
more than having 10 will.

Another thing to be aware of is that even though some tri-merge
credit reports only show 90 days' worth of inquiries, they do still
include the additional nine months' worth of inquiries in the score.
A tri-merge credit report contains all three bureaus within one con-
densed credit report. It is the format primarily used by mortgage
lenders. The score is actually calculated at the credit bureau before
the data is passed on to the tri-merge company. In fact, a lot of
things don't show up on the credit report you get, but it doesn't mean
the information was not ever there; it just means that the company
compiling your credit report didn't print out all of the information
sent to it from the bureaus. Nevertheless, your score will still reflect
the information you don't see because the score is generated from
the complete data in the bureau's records, not whatever incomplete
information you see on the printed report. This does not mean that
every credit report you see is incomplete, it just means that there is
a chance that your score is possibly based on data you are not aware
of. Some credit reports have complete information and some don't,

but the score is always generated from the complete data stored in the bureau's database.

Tips for this category:

✓ Inquiries affect the score for one year.

✓ Inquiries can cost anywhere from 0 to 50 points per inquiry, although 5 points per inquiry is the average I've seen.

✓ It's possible that the credit score is only reduced for approximately the first 10 inquiries—but this number is not 100% certain, so assume every inquiry counts.

✓ Auto and mortgage inquiries:

> ➤ have a 30-day buffer period before the score is affected.

> ➤ all made within a 45-day period are treated, for scoring purposes, as one inquiry per loan category (auto vs. mortgage)

✓ Many inquiries don't count, such as:

> ➤ personal

> ➤ promotional and job related

> ➤ insurance, utilities, housing

> ➤ account reviews

Summing It Up

That pretty much covers the factors used in determining your credit score. Let's do a quick recap:

1. How you pay your bills: on time is good, late is bad

2. How much you owe your creditors in relation to your limits, primarily on your revolving credit cards: keep your credit card debt low (less than 10% utilization is optimal)

3. How long you've had credit: the longer the better

4. Account mix: diversity is good

5. How often you apply for credit: apply only when you really need it

Adhering to these five key principles will get you well on your way to healthy credit and a stellar credit score.

NEXT STEPS:
WHAT YOU CAN DO TO IMPROVE A POOR SCORE

Now that you understand a bit about what goes into a credit report and credit score, and see what ills yours is suffering from, you're ready to take the next step in doing something about it.

Over the next two chapters, we're going to be addressing how to reduce the negatives that are being reported against you and harming your score, and increase those things that reflect positively on your report and improve your score.

If you follow the advice I'm going to give you, your score will have no choice but to improve. Remember, poor credit scores are only indicative of the information being reported in your credit reports. If you can remove inaccurate items, manage your credit, and change your negative credit patterns, you will positively impact your score.

4

"Repairing" Your Damaged Credit

Credit repair isn't rocket science. If your score is low, it's usually because your credit report contains too many negatives bringing the score down and not enough positives to bring the score up. Other symptoms may be high revolving debt or not much credit on your report, period. Although there are subtleties to knowing precisely what to attack with the resources you've got, and when, the general credit repair strategy comes down to three main steps:

1. Remove or change items that are lowering your score.

2. Pay down revolving debt to lower your utilization.

3. Add items that will increase your score.

We'll address the first of these strategies in detail in this chapter. The next two strategies will be covered in Chapter 5.

THE ART OF THE DISPUTE

In Chapter 2 we learned about the many ways inaccurate information can get on your credit report. Effective credit repair requires that you dispute negative items on your credit report that you have deemed to be inaccurate. And as we discussed in Chapter 2, the process for disputing inaccurate or incomplete items on your credit report starts with sending dispute letters to the credit bureaus telling them that an item is inaccurate, giving a dispute reason (in what way it is inaccurate), and asking the CRAs to therefore delete the item from your credit report or correct it to reflect accurate reporting.

Per the FCRA, the credit bureau is required to perform an investigation on your behalf to ensure that your credit report does not contain inaccurate information. To do this, they contact the creditor and ask them to verify the accuracy of the information on your report. But, as we also learned in Chapter 2, the CRAs' investigation amounts to a tortured reading of the FCRA on a good day and a crime against humanity on a bad day. They merely process the disputes without an investigation, entering them into their computer using dispute codes that rarely communicate the entirety of your dispute points and then send them on to the different creditors, who also will rarely do a thorough investigation into the incomplete gripe they received from the credit bureaus on your behalf.

The only way to counteract the bureau not truly communicating your dispute is to send the dispute directly to the creditor yourself. Even then, the creditor will usually not do anything other than read their computer screen to determine if an error was made. Given the daunting amount of work that goes into contacting each individual creditor, I suggest disputing only with the bureaus with the hope that the creditor will not answer in the required 30-day time frame, in which case the item must be deleted or changed according to the claims you made in your letter to the bureaus asking them to dispute it initially. Then at least you don't have to worry about their lack of attention to your request because you'll get the result you asked for even if they blatantly overlook certain details you bring to their attention. Remember, with credit repair, it's the result you care about, not the road it took to get there.

Types of Derogatories Hurting Your Score

The following chart lists the different types of derogatory items that may be hurting your score. In this chapter, we will discuss each of these and how to best approach getting them removed from the credit report. But first, let's look at how long each derogatory naturally stays on the credit report.

DELINQUENCY	TIME ON CREDIT REPORT
Late Payments	7 years from the time the late payment occurred
Charge-Offs	7.5 years from first late payment that led to the charge-off (though in the real world it comes off only 7 years, not 7.5 as the law allows)
Collection Accounts	7 years from the date of first delinquency with the original creditor the collector is collecting for. (Please note that selling a collection to a new collector does not allow the new collector to report for an additional 7 years. They must still remove the account from the report after 7 years. While this is the law, the fact remains that re-aging is a violation done by collectors on a daily basis.)
Repossessions	7 years from the time the car was repossessed. Keep in mind that a deficiency balance may be owed once the bank sells the car at auction, which explains why many repossession accounts show a balance owing.
Foreclosures	7 years from the time the foreclosure was initiated

DELINQUENCY	TIME ON CREDIT REPORT
Bankruptcies:	
Chapter 7 & 11	10 years from the filing date
Chapter 13	10 years from the filing date, although some bureaus remove it after 7 as an internal policy. The law allows them to keep it there for 10 years, if they so choose.
Tax Liens	7 years from date satisfied; up to 15 years if unpaid seems to be when they fall off the report, even though the FCRA allows the CRAs to report them indefinitely if they remain unpaid.
Judgments	Depends on state: 7 years or the statute of limitations (SOL) for that state, although the CRAs remove them after 7 years from the date the judgment was entered.
Inquiries	2 years from the date of the inquiry, even though the FICO® score will not score inquiries older than 12 months.

New York State Residents Only (must be current resident)

- Satisfied judgments cannot remain on your credit file longer than 5 years from the date paid.
- Paid collections remain on your credit file no longer than 5 years from the date paid.

California State Residents Only (must be current resident)

- Paid or released tax liens remain on your credit file for 7 years from the date released or 10 years from the date filed.
- Unpaid or unreleased tax liens remain on your credit file for 10 years from the file date.

What to Target on a Credit Report

Successfully disputing derogatories has its ins and outs, which can only be learned from experience. I have personally spent years and hundreds of thousands of dollars trying different approaches in learning what works and what doesn't. Because each person's credit history is unique with its own set of details, a great deal of strategy is needed about exactly what to dispute and when to dispute it in order to maximize a score. Factors include the age of delinquency, the number of delinquencies, how many points you need to increase your score to get approved for a loan, and much more. Following are some general tips based on my discoveries and success with thousands of clients over the years.

- Look at the scores first. What is the middle score and what do you need that middle score to be in order to get approved for a loan? (This is assuming you are currently trying to get a loan. If you are just trying to get your score as high as possible, this is not something you need to analyze too much.)

- Look at the reason codes to see what the biggest problems are. (Why did this person score less than the maximum possible score of 850? That's what the reason codes are meant to tell you.) The biggest reason you scored less than 850 is listed on top under each score, with the second highest reason below that, the third below that, and so on.

- Payment history makes up 35% of the score, so the more delinquencies that are removed, the better the score will be. Keep in mind, too, that the older the delinquency, the less it affects your score. I've seen people with a 4-year-old bankruptcy who had a 720 credit score. They had tons of good credit to drown out the bankruptcy, but the main reason for the 720 score was that the BK was old and the positive credit was abundant. Sometimes, disputing an inaccurate older account can lead to the creditor updating it with more recent inaccurate information that hurts the score even more. This is something you need to be prepared for, because it occurs too much of the time.

Items That Don't Hurt Your Score

Some questionable-looking items appearing on your credit report do not actually hurt your score. Therefore, even if these items are incorrect or inaccurate, you should not waste your time or effort disputing them. For example, "Card lost" does not hurt the credit score. It may indicate that you are more of a fraud risk and penalize you that way, but it doesn't hurt the score. Other harmless items include:

- Social Security number security checks

- I-U: this code means unknown status. If this account is negative, it may not be worth opening a can of worms that will end up hurting your score instead of helping it. You don't want to turn a neutral into a negative.

- "Unknown Account": Sometimes you will see an account listed on your credit report that has an account number but the creditor name says "unknown." Even though it says "unknown," the CRA will know which creditor the account is reported by since they decide who reports to them and whose data they will accept. Therefore, this is not something that can be used to your advantage in at attempt to get the account deleted.

Credit Repair Success with Removing Negative Items

So, what's the likelihood of getting something removed? The truth is: it varies. With credit repair, there are no guarantees. I go by the law of averages. Even if an item (for example, a particular retail store account) gets removed four times in a row for four different clients of mine, on the fifth time it may not work. The success of credit repair is largely dependent on how the other side handles your dispute.

We're relying on the credit bureaus, the creditors, and the collection agencies to either do or not do their job, and we never know just how well they will show up and investigate and/or fight the dispute. We count on them not being organized enough to respond in the 30-day time limit or with enough information to contradict our dispute. We're hoping they won't respond, or that something will get screwed up in the paperwork on their end. But sometimes, when something should be a slam dunk, it hits a quagmire that can't be explained.

To your benefit as a consumer, creditors may not have access to their complete set of records, they may have purged their records to make space for new business, so they may give you the benefit of the doubt and delete the item or not respond to the credit bureaus at all, which accomplishes the same. That's what we're hoping for, the easiest way to get you from point A to point B. We already know that they are not going to competently handle the request to remove or change the information that you are telling them is inaccurate, so whether it gets removed by a thorough investigation or through the ball being dropped on their end, who cares!

That's why you have to be clever with your dispute to make sure that if they aren't going to do their job, you will at least have more than one chance to start their dispute-process machine with the hope that it will break down in your favor. If you have a negative account on your credit report that is inaccurate for any reason, you'll want to dispute it.

Guidelines for a Successful Dispute

A seasoned credit repair organization will have learned over the years what dispute reasons have been most effective at getting an item removed. They will use the best argument they know to be effective at getting the CRAs' attention so that the CRAs are forced to do their job in verifying the accuracy of the item, or delete it. Following are some guidelines I use for getting the best results with a dispute.

- As mentioned, send your letter directly to the CRAs only, rather than also to the individual creditors. Sending to creditors is much more work and will not dramatically increase results; in fact, in some circumstances this may decrease your success by preventing the bureau from making a mistake in your favor that they would have made had you disputed with the bureaus only.

- Assuming you are going to dispute with the bureaus only, you want to supply along with your first dispute letter a photocopy of your Social Security card (to prove your Social Security number) and a copy of your driver's license (to prove your mailing address); otherwise, the CRAs may kick your dispute back to you and ask you to prove your identity. This is only needed if your current address is not on the credit reports you are looking at when writing your dispute letters. Other forms of acceptable proof for your Social Security number include a pay-stub with your Social Security number on it, the front page of your 1040, or a 1099. Valid forms of proving your address other than a driver's license are a utility bill, a bank statement, a lease agreement, or if all else fails and you have none of those with your current address listed, a notarized affidavit claiming your address is your address! Note that you are supposed to prove your current *mailing address*, not your residence (unless, of course, that is your mailing address too). Having a P.O. Box as a mailing address is perfectly acceptable and the credit bureaus will mail your reports there provided you send them the proof required to verify that it is you with that mailing address.

- If the CRA does not agree to remove the inaccurate item after the first letter, you need to send another letter with stronger language and more detailed explanations of why they need to delete. In other words, the dispute escalates. This progression is important. You don't want to give your best reason away at first, because then you would have nowhere to go from there. So, the second letter needs to increase in tone and verbiage. This is crucial because sending several letters that merely say the same thing will only allow the CRA or lender to say "previously verified" and dismiss your dispute. Nor do you want to contradict yourself, as this might lead them to question the credibility of your dispute and deem the claim "frivolous." The FCRA allows credit bureaus to disregard disputes they believe to be "frivolous." You will want to send up to three or four dispute letters before giving up.

- Despite popular belief, having a legally worded dispute letter—meaning one that sounds "official" or like a lawyer drafted it—

is not always the best approach when dealing with the credit bureaus. I've found that, above all else, keeping it simple works best. The language in the letter should be such that anyone can understand it, quickly and easily.

- Starting out, you'll want to say as little as possible to try to get something removed. If their response is that they have "verified" the account or item, then you need to increase the language in the next letter, but still leave some ammunition in reserve for a third and fourth letter. Different people at the CRAs and creditors take in the dispute letters, and some will be more lenient than others.

- You'll know if an item has been deleted when you get your new credit reports from the CRAs. If the item has not been removed, send another letter that escalates in language/verbiage. Again, after four letters, it's probably time to give up.

Sample Flowchart and Dispute Letters

Following are a sample dispute letter flowchart for a "single" 30-day late payment and four sample letters showing how the dispute language/verbiage should escalate. Keep in mind that these are not "one size fits all" and there are hundreds of possible approaches depending on the individual facts surrounding your dispute. These samples represent only one plausible approach; each dispute needs to be determined on a case-by-case basis because every credit report is unique.

The flow of the sample dispute is explained on the following pages:

First Letter

The dispute reason is:

I was not 30 days late on this account in October 2007

- The reason you want to give a specific month here is to allow yourself the opportunity to contact them again if this letter is not successful and still have other scenarios you can ask them to address. If you say, "I was never late on this account," you are unnecessarily painting yourself into a corner by eliminating the ability to change your story without looking like you are saying something completely different. You want to give the bureaus as little information as possible in order to get them to open the dispute. Save other small details for future letters so you don't contradict yourself by giving them too many details on the first letter.

Second Letter
(if first letter didn't work)

The dispute reason is:

I was not 30 days late on this account during the month listed; please specifically validate with the creditor the accuracy of this information and update my account accordingly.

- Here you are essentially saying the same thing you said in the first letter, but you are casting a wider net and changing the language slightly without contradicting yourself.

Third Letter
(if second letter didn't work)
The dispute reason is:

Customer Service agreed to give me a courtesy adjustment under the circumstances; please verify this with them and remove the 30-day late payment on my report.

- The first two letters pretty much exhausted the "this information is incorrect" approach, so here the language switches focus from the accuracy to the agreement made by Customer Service.

Fourth Letter
(if third letter didn't work)
The dispute reason is:

Why is there still a 30-day late payment showing on my report? Remove this immediately or I'll hire an attorney to deal with this.

- This is your "Hail Mary" attempt, which they may or may not blow off, but it is worth the try. If this doesn't work, I suggest either giving up until the item comes off on its own or investing time calling the actual creditor if your story (as to what happened with the account that led to the 30-day late payment being reported) is half decent and you feel you can get the right support representative for the creditor to change the reporting.

Now that you understand why it is important to give as little information as possible in order to increase the chances that future disputes will not be rejected as easily by the bureaus, let's take a look at how the sample letter to the bureaus would look using the example flowchart above.

Sample First Letter

To: All Three Credit Bureaus

From: John Doe
        123 Main St.
        Somewhere, CA 90001
        SS# 123-45-6789

January 1, 2011

To whom it may concern:

In reference to XYZ Creditor with Account # 4271221122334433 showing on my credit report, please note that I was not 30 days late on this account in October 2007. Please remove that information and send me an updated credit report. I am including a copy of my pay-stub and a utility bill with my name on it to prove both my Social Security number and my mailing address.

Sincerely,

John Doe

Sample Second Letter (if needed)

To: All Three Credit Bureaus

From: John Doe
123 Main St.
Somewhere, CA 90001
SS# 123-45-6789

February 12, 2011

To whom it may concern:

In reference to XYZ Creditor with Account # 4271221122334433 showing on my credit report, I was not 30 days late on this account during the month listed; please specifically validate with the creditor the accuracy of this information and update my account accordingly and send me an updated credit report once completed.

Sincerely,

John Doe

Sample Third Letter (if needed)

To: All Three Credit Bureaus

From: John Doe
123 Main St.
Somewhere, CA 90001
SS# 123-45-6789

March 23, 2011

To whom it may concern:

In reference to XYZ Creditor with Account # 4271221122334433 showing on my credit report, customer service agreed to give me a courtesy adjustment under the circumstances. Please verify this with them and remove the 30-day late payment on my report.

Sincerely,

John Doe

Sample Fourth Letter (if needed)

To: All Three Credit Bureaus

From: John Doe
123 Main St.
Somewhere, CA 90001
SS# 123-45-6789

May 7, 2011

To whom it may concern:

In reference to XYZ Creditor with Account # 4271221122334433 showing on my credit report, why is there still a 30-day late payment showing on my report? Remove this immediately or I'll hire an attorney to deal with this.

Sincerely,

John Doe

Keep a record of your dispute letters. Create a file for each of your individual credit reports (on each CRA), as well as for each specific creditor you are disputing to directly if you decide to go that route.

Getting a Response

The CRA will send your dispute to the creditor or collection agency and wait for a response. Once again, to reiterate, if you use the same exact wording in the dispute letters each time you send a dispute, the CRAs will likely say that the disputed information was "previously verified." You want to send letters that are going to trigger a new investigation without looking contradictory or frivolous, as demonstrated in the sample flowchart and letters above. Don't eat the whole pie in the first sitting if you want to have four days of dessert! The CRAs will keep your disputes on record for at least six months.

Even if a credit bureau does not respond to a dispute within 30 days (or 45 days if the dispute was initiated from a *www.AnnualCreditReport.com* credit report), they do *not* have to remove the disputed item forever; they just need to remove it until the creditor responds back to them. Once the creditor verifies the account, the credit bureaus can reinsert the item on your credit report provided they notify you within five days of doing so.

Some Credit Repair Myths about Disputes

Some books on credit repair will warn you not to dispute too many items at the same time, as this may indicate to the CRAs that your claims are frivolous. I disagree. You can dispute everything at once; it won't hurt you. If you want to dispute 10 items, you or the credit repair clinic you hire can go after all 10 at once. In my decade of being a credit repair expert, I have tried this both ways: sending out 10 individual letters and sending out one letter with 10 items, and the only difference in the outcome was a lot more paperwork when sending out individual letters for each dispute, as every dispute created a new credit report being sent back to my clients. I also tried to dispute only one or two items each month, which just took longer to get from point A to point B with the same result at the end of the day.

The CRAs may not look favorably on this practice of submitting many items at once, but I have found that it does not harm the chance of credit repair because the credit bureaus can't assume a dispute is frivolous just because there are a lot of items. Many people do have numerous inaccurate items on their report, and the bureaus have no way of knowing which are legit and which are not—and if they label the wrong person's letter as frivolous, they run the risk of being sued. As noted, if a consumer goes through the proper channels of the dispute process and gets no results at having an inaccurate item corrected or removed, the consumer can sue the CRA—the penalty to the CRA being $1,000 plus attorney's fees if they lose.

Another credit repair myth is that you have to send certified letters to the CRAs. I have found that the credit bureaus are good at receiving disputes, and certifying the delivery of the letters is simply not necessary with them unless your main intent from the start is to sue, in which case it is a good idea to build your case file in regards to the evidence being stronger.

The creditors and collection agencies, on the other hand, are bad at responding; dispute letters to them should *always* be certified if you plan on disputing directly with them in addition to the bureaus.

Disputing with the Big Banks

Be aware that the big banks never agree to delete anything, no matter how much you dispute it. When dealing with them directly, if you don't have a really good reason, don't waste your time. They operate like robots, where everything must follow their system. The clerks processing disputes simply don't have the authority or flexibility to handle any requests outside of their standard practices. They love to hide behind the phrase "Sorry, but it is not a bank error." *But Mr. Big Bank Peon, I was run over by a bus as I was opening the blue mailbox to drop in my payment to you and went into a six-month coma, and that's why you didn't get a payment.* "Sorry, it was not a bank error and we can't help you." UGH!!! It's this reason alone that you want to only go to the credit bureaus for items on which your position is weak, because the bureaus have soft spots that can be

75

exploited to your benefit while the big banks are akin to Fort Knox on these types of requests.

TYPES OF DEROGATORIES TO ATTEMPT TO REMOVE—EITHER BY DISPUTE OR BY SETTLEMENT

When we talk about removing negative items from the credit report, we're primarily dealing with poor payment history in the form of late payments and defaulting on loans in the form of charge-offs, collections, judgments, repossessions, foreclosures, and bankruptcies. Obviously, these different types of derogatories vary in severity and therefore also vary in how challenging they are to get removed.

Following is information on each type of negative item, along with some tips to be aware of in dealing with them in the credit repair process. Some items you will be successful in getting deleted through the dispute letter process; others will be better resolved by paying a settlement to have them deleted from the credit report or to otherwise boost your score.

Late Payments

Before going through the dispute letter process outlined earlier, contact all creditors that report late payments of 30 days on your credit report and request a "good faith adjustment" that removes the late payments reported on your account. Getting them to agree to 60 days or more is almost impossible and not worth the effort. If at first they refuse to remove the late payments, be persistent and remind them that you have been a good customer and would deeply appreciate their help. Since most creditors receive calls within a call center, if one representative refuses to make a courtesy adjustment on your account, call back and try again with someone else. Persistence and politeness pay off in this scenario. If you are frustrated, rude, and unclear with your request, then you are making it very difficult for them to want to help you.

Within the delinquent accounts on your credit report, there is a column called "Past Due." Credit scoring software penalizes you for keeping accounts past due. Past Dues destroy a credit score. If you see an amount in this column, pay the creditor the past due amount reported to bring the account current. Definitely pay items that are 150 days late to avoid charge-off status because once the account goes to charge-off or collection status, the only way to bring the account current is to pay it in full.

Student Loans

You always want to settle and pay government student loans, no matter how old. The reasons it's important are:

1. If the student loans are guaranteed by the government, you can't bankrupt them (unless extreme hardship is proven, which is almost impossible—like being in a coma).

2. It will be at least 25 years, if not forever, of your not paying before they write it off. They can take your income tax overpayments if you don't pay, and there is nothing in the FCRA that prohibits them from reporting for a longer period beyond 7 years like most accounts. If possible, try to take advantage of any rehabilitation programs that the student loan lender has available. Ask them if they have a rehabilitation program and if you qualify for it. A rehabilitation program is a program for delinquent student loan debtors, where the debtor has to make payments on time for a year, and then they will remove the derogatory payment history from the credit reports after the payments are made on-time for 9 months straight. If you pay off the loan earlier than 9 months, they don't delete it from the credit report, so make sure to only pay the minimum payment they require so you do not pay off the loan before the 9 months is up.

Student loans also seem to split and spread, separating into different accounts on the credit report, which harms the score considerably. They jump around from collector to collector, or whoever is working on the account. These accounts are notorious for duplicate reporting and should be reviewed carefully to assure they are being reported correctly. But remember, just because you see eight student loan accounts for $10,000 each, it does not automatically mean that the account is a duplicate. Many student loans are a set amount given twice a year to the student for 4 years of college. This would mean that it is possible to have eight different loans with the same loan amount that are not duplication errors.

A Note about Duplicate or Split Accounts
Duplicate or "split" accounts—whether student loans or other types of accounts—will sometimes have slightly different account numbers with all of the information being the same except one digit in the account number. This is usually the creditor playing games on the credit report and it hurts your credit score because the scoring software treats them as though they are separate delinquent accounts. Always dispute duplicates or split accounts as "Not mine." If that doesn't work, dispute them as "duplicates."

Sometimes you'll see "Transferred" on an account on your credit report. When positive, this often occurs when one creditor is bought out by another. When negative, it often occurs when a debt is sold to another collection agency. As I stated earlier, with the exception of a judgment that resulted from the debt, there should never be more than two listings for one account that has been sold: the original account and the latest collection agency. If the middleman is on there, dispute it to have it removed. Otherwise, you are being penalized too many times.

Judgments
Judgments are considered major derogatories by the credit score and have the same effect on the credit score as any 90-day or more late payment, any settlement, any collection, lien, or even a bankruptcy! Since all credit reports are different, you can't assign a certain point value to each derogatory, but assume that a major derogatory will hurt the score up to 200 points depending on how high the score is and how much room the score has to drop in addition to everything else that makes that credit report unique. The higher the score, the more of an effect a major derogatory will have on the score. That's because, as you know, the purpose of the score is to indicate the likelihood of a consumer going 90 days late on a loan within the next 24 months. If they've had a good score but suddenly suffer a

major derogatory, it makes sense that their score will fall dramatically, indicating a new risk. If someone with a 480 credit score files a bankruptcy, their score might only go down 20 points because they already have a very low score indicating their likelihood to default. When a score is low, it just can't be hurt all that much more.

If you dispute the accuracy of a judgment and the public record reporting company either agrees with you or doesn't respond to the dispute letter, then the item gets deleted or changed to what you claim is accurate. If the public record reporting company replies to the bureaus that the item is accurate, it won't get changed at all.

The good news is that I have found that if judgments come off the credit report through the dispute process, they don't come back on, even if they're unpaid.

One last thing to keep in mind is that although judgments fall off the credit report after 7 years, that doesn't mean they can't be collected on even after that time. They can be collected on until they are paid.

Repossessions & Foreclosures

Repossessions and foreclosures affect the score the same as any other major derogatory and can be removed by disputing their accuracy, similar to the process mentioned in judgments above.

Bankruptcies

Everyone knows that bankruptcies are bad for a credit score, but the truth is that the BK itself has the same effect on the score as any other major derogatory. The reason it's more damaging overall is because all of the accounts that were included in the bankruptcy are, individually, additional major derogatories. Thus, though the bankruptcy by itself has the same score deduction effect as a 90-day late payment—no more, no less—a BK has the potential of seriously polluting a credit report if a number of accounts were written off in the BK.

So, can credit repair help someone with a BK? While, bankruptcies themselves are very hard to get off all three CRAs, you can still benefit from credit repair because it is possible to get the accounts included in BK removed successfully. Since, as I've said, these are each major derogatories, the score will increase as a result of getting them removed. So the answer is YES, you can benefit from credit repair if you have a BK, just don't expect the BK itself to come off because they rarely do. The accounts included in BK are easier to get removed, though, and the benefit will come from that.

Keep in mind that bankruptcies can stay on the credit report for 10 years from the filing date and that this still holds true even if the person initiates a bankruptcy but then fails to follow through on it. Also keep in mind that a Chapter 7 BK wipes out the debt, but Chapter 13 does not. With Chapter 13, it takes up to three years to pay off the debt, so balances will show on a Chapter 13 until the repayment period is over and the final discharge is entered by the judge. Therefore, if you're lucky enough to get a Chapter 13 BK deleted from your credit report, there's a good chance it will show up again with different numbers as it gets updated and re-reported during the repayment plan process.

Accounts included in a Chapter 7 BK should not show a balance. If they do, send a first dispute letter saying, "This account is inaccurate." If they won't correct it, say, "This account is mine, but it was included in BK and should have a zero balance."

The main thing to keep in mind is that a BK is hard to get off. With the items included in the BK, however, there's a lot of room for improving the credit score, in many cases up to 100 points, if you're lucky. There are usually a lot of inaccurate negative items—balances owed, etc.—that can be deleted to improve the score.

Inquiries

Inquiries do not affect the credit score much at all, in most cases an average of 5 points per inquiry although this number, as noted previously, can be anywhere from 0 to 50 points depending on the rest of the person's credit report.

If you dispute an inquiry as being inaccurate because you never agreed to have the lender pull your credit, the chances of your getting it removed are hit or miss because the bureaus usually blow off your dispute and reply that inquiries are a matter of record. Therefore, the best way I have found to dispute it is, "It is not mine," or, "I did not inquire with XX Lender on [date]." Only write two letters then give up on it. Inquiries only make up 10% of the credit score, and my experience has been that it is not worth the time to dispute them. The thicker the credit file, the less inquiries affect the score.

Charge-Offs & Collections

I've saved charge-offs and collections as the last types of derogatories to discuss because they are much more involved than the others to get removed. The first things you need to understand on this topic are your rights when dealing with debt collectors and what a statute of limitations (SOL) is.

YOUR RIGHTS IN DEALING WITH DEBT COLLECTORS

A debt collector is a person or firm hired to collect the money you owe to an original creditor, whether that creditor be a bank, a judgment creditor, or a dentist who says you didn't pay for your root canal. For years, debt collectors were notorious for their perfidious behavior in trying to get consumers to pay their debts. As a response, the Fair Debt Collection Practices Act (FDCPA) was added in 1978 as a statute of the Consumer Credit Protection Act for the primary purpose of putting a stop to the underhanded and abusive tactics practiced by many debt collectors against consumers.

The FDCPA specifically covers consumer debts that are being collected by a third-party collector. Therefore, the original creditor does not have to abide by the FDCPA, nor does a third-party collector that is collecting business-related debts. The FDCPA only applies to collectors of personal, family, and household debts, including car loans, mortgages, charge accounts, and medical bills.

The FDCPA establishes guidelines for how debt collectors can legally conduct themselves when trying to collect these debts, and states the rights of consumers when dealing with debt collectors. It also outlines penalties and remedies for debt collectors who violate these guidelines.

As an example, within five days after a debt collector first contacts you, the collector must mail you a notice detailing the name of the creditor, the amount you owe, and instructions on what to do if you believe you do not owe the debt. This is known in industry terms as the "dunning letter."

Also, under the FDCPA, a debt collector cannot:

- Contact you at unreasonable times, for example, before 8 a.m. or after 9 p.m., unless you agree

- Contact you at work if you tell the debt collector your employer doesn't allow it

- Contact you after you write a letter asking them to stop, except to notify you that they or the creditor is planning to sue you to collect on the debt or is calling to tell you they no longer plan on pursuing the debt

- Contact the people in your life—your friends, relatives, employer, or others—except to get information about where you live and work

- Harass you by threatening you harm, using profane language, or calling you repeatedly

- Make claims that you will be arrested or make any other untrue statements

- Threaten to garnish your wages or file a lawsuit against you unless they or the creditor actually intends to do so and if doing so would be legal because the statute of limitations (SOL) has not yet run out

The best thing to do when contacted by a collection agency is to hang up and walk away without a conversation. If you need to file a complaint against a debt collector, contact your state or local consumer protection agency and the Federal Trade Commission.

Federal Trade Commission
Bureau of Consumer Protection
Consumer Response Center
600 Pennsylvania Ave., NW
Washington, DC 20580
Toll-Free: 1-877-FTC-HELP (382-4357)
TTY: 1-866-653-4261 (Toll-Free)
www.ftc.gov

What a Statute of Limitations (SOL) Is & How It Works

Creditors and debt collectors have a limited time window in which to sue debtors for nonpayment of credit obligations once the borrower defaults on that obligation. That limit is set by a statute of limitations (SOL). The SOL period varies by state and also varies depending on if the debt resulted from a written contract, an oral contract, a promissory note, or an open account. To determine which state governs your particular situation, you need to assess two things: 1) Which state did you live in when you entered into the agreement with the creditor? and 2) Which state do you reside in now?

This is important because the SOL periods can vary dramatically between states. Kentucky, for example, has a 15-year SOL on written contracts while California's SOL for written contracts is 4 years. So, if you lived in Kentucky when you got the credit card but now live in California, the creditor will be allowed to choose which state's law governs as to the SOL. Which state do you think the creditor will choose? Kentucky, of course! If, however, you lived in California both when you entered into the contract with the creditor and remained there until now, you know that they only have 4 years to sue you from the time you breached the agreement, which started to tick the first day you were late on the account and that late payment also eventually led to a charge-off without your bringing the account current before it was charged off. In this example, once the clock reaches 4 years, you are golden—they cannot successfully sue you because you have an SOL defense.

The chart on page 85 gives you the statute of limitations for each state as it pertains to the different types of contracts the person has with their creditors. Here is an example of each type of contract:

Oral – A contract that was agreed to verbally with no written agreement. This would be the case when you lend a friend $100 and he agrees to pay you back within 30 days.

Written – A contract between two or more parties where the terms of what the parties are agreeing to are on paper and signed by all of the parties involved. An example of this would be a mortgage loan or a car loan. One could even make an argument that a credit card Terms of Service Agreement that states that the consumer agrees to the new updated terms for using the card every time they sign for a new charge is a written agreement. (Although the proper way to classify a credit card is as an open-ended account, it doesn't prevent the bank from arguing that the account is written if it serves their interest in court for having a longer SOL. For this reason, you need to always defend yourself if being sued to assure that your rights are protected. If you don't assert your rights, the other side will get away with painting the picture that serves their purpose.)

Promissory – A promise to pay a specified amount on demand or at a certain time. In credit situations, this usually comes up in the form of a co-signer, where the co-signer agrees to pay the defaulted balance on demand if the primary borrower defaults on the terms.

Open-Ended Account – A loan with no fixed terms. A revolving credit card is called open-ended credit because the length of the loan isn't fixed—it's ongoing. The two most important terms of a revolving credit loan are the line of credit and the interest rate. Once a person pays down the balance, they are allowed to re-borrow up to the limit placed on the account.

STATUTE OF LIMITATIONS

State	Oral	Written	Promissory	Open-Ended Accounts
AL	6	6	6	3
AR	5	5	5	3
AK	6	6	3	3
AZ	3	6	6	3
CA	2	4	4	4
CO	6	6	6	3
CT	3	6	6	3
DE	3	3	3	4
DC	3	3	3	3
FL	4	5	5	4
GA	4	6	6	4
HI	6	6	6	6
IA	5	10	5	5
ID	4	5	5	4
IL	5	10	10	5
IN	6	10	10	6
KS	3	6	5	3
KY	5	15	15	5
LA	10	10	10	3
ME	6	6	6	6
MD	3	3	6	3
MA	6	6	6	6
MI	6	6	6	6
MN	6	6	6	6
MS	3	3	3	3
MO	5	10	10	5
MT	3	8	8	5
NC	3	3	5	3
ND	6	6	6	6
NE	4	5	5	4
NH	3	3	6	3
NJ	6	6	6	3
NM	4	6	6	4
NV	4	6	3	4
NY	6	6	6	6
OH	6	15	15	6
OK	3	5	5	3
OR	6	6	6	6
PA	4	4	4	4
RI	10	5	6	4
SC	3	3	3	3
SD	6	6	6	6
TN	6	6	6	3
TX	4	4	4	4
UT	4	6	6	4
VA	3	5	6	3
VT	6	6	5	3
WA	3	6	6	3
WI	6	6	10	6
WV	5	10	6	5
WY	8	10	10	8

85

Time-Barred Debt

Debts that remain unpaid beyond the SOL are often referred to as "time-barred debts." While debt collectors can still try to collect time-barred debts, they are not allowed to use the courts to do so.

But, believe it or not, this doesn't mean that they won't sue you and try to collect it through the courts; it just means that you will win if you raise an SOL defense. You still need to defend yourself, because if you don't, you will lose. To win, you must show up in court and raise your defense. So, whatever you do, don't ignore those court notices about your old debts! You don't want to lose a case that could have easily been thrown out of court if you only showed up and defended yourself with an SOL defense.

When calculating the SOL, remember that most credit card contracts are considered either written or open, even if applied for by phone because the Terms of Service Agreement states that you agree to the terms in writing every time you use your card and sign the charge slip.

Also, be sure that you do not confuse the statute of limitations on a debt with the length of time the debt can remain on your credit report according to the FCRA. These are two separate issues. For example, a charged-off credit card account in California may have an SOL of 4 years, but will remain on the credit report for up to 7.5 years. A bankruptcy can stay on a credit report for 10 years, regardless of the statute of limitations.

Debt Validation

Third-party collection agencies have to jump through more hoops than original creditors do when complying with the law; one of those hoops is called "debt validation." Burden of proof is higher for a collection agency than the original creditor thanks to the Fair Debt Collection Practices Act (FDCPA). Third-party collectors must validate a debt when the consumer asks them to, if the consumer requests that validation during the first 30 days from when the initial dunning letter is sent to the consumer by the collector.

As mentioned, the dunning letter is the first letter the collection agency sends the consumer—it states the amount that they owe and that the debt is assumed to be valid unless the consumer disputes the debt within 30 days. The consumer needs to dispute the debt in writing at that time before the 30 days expires; otherwise, the collection agency is not legally bound to validate that the debt is owed by the consumer. After the 30 days has passed, the collection agency only has to prove that they mailed the initial dunning letter. They don't even have to prove that the debtor received it—only that it was mailed. The good news is that most collection agencies *do not know* that they are not required to validate the debt after the 30 days expires, and they will attempt to validate the letter anyway if the debtor requests so.

A debt validation letter is a simple letter that asks the debt collector to provide validation of this debt by sending you sufficient evidence (not a computer printout from their screen, but *proof* that you owe the debt and are obligated to pay the debt). If you send the collection agency a request to validate the debt and they do not provide you with sufficient proof within those first 30 days, then their reporting of that debt to the credit bureaus after the 30 days expires would be in violation of federal law. If, however, they validate the debt at a later date, they can then legally report the account to the credit bureaus.

When an older collection account is sold around to different collection agencies, it's usually just the data that is sold, not the original documentation on the account, so it's much harder for the collection agency to prove that the debt belongs to the consumer. Often, therefore, the collection agency will be unable to properly validate the debt as required by the FDCPA. The older it is, and the more times it has been sold to other agencies, the more likely they won't have the documentation to prove it's yours. In cases like this, it should be easier to get the collection agency to delete their derogatory account from your credit report.

If the collection agency just ignores your letter demanding validation of your debt, you should send the next one as a certified letter. If they still ignore you, document that you sent the letters asking for validation of the item, say they were non-responsive, and give all of that information to the credit bureaus and ask them to remove the item if it has been reported on your credit report. Note, however, that a collection agency is usually *not* able to get the original creditor to delete their listing on the credit report, so don't expect that you will accomplish getting both the collection and the original charge-off deleted. Chances are, it won't happen.

Unpaid collections are tricky and shouldn't be disputed through the credit bureaus like other derogatories can be. The main reason you shouldn't dispute unpaid collections (unless they are both beyond the SOL and at least 4 years old) is because even if you're lucky enough to get an unpaid collection or charge-off deleted, it will usually reappear.

The FCRA requires the credit bureau to inform the consumer in writing if they re-insert a credit account that was removed previously due to the creditor not responding within 30 days from the date of the dispute. Usually, if an item is going to reappear, it will reappear within 60 days of its being removed, but if the debt is unpaid it will almost always reappear as long as it is within the 7-year reporting period. This is because the creditor wants to be paid, and reporting an unpaid debt to the bureaus will increase those chances significantly. That's why it is good to try to settle newer collections when you can because once the collection is paid or settled, the collector rarely re-reports the item. They use the credit reporting system as leverage to get you to pay, so once it's been paid, what would be the point?

The Effects of Charge-Offs and Collection Accounts on the Credit Score

When older than 24 months, charge-offs and collections do not affect your credit score nearly as much as they do when less than 24 months. In fact, they're probably only hurting you for about 20 points each at the 2-year mark. Therefore, paying an older charge-off or collection will not significantly help your score, although you do get a slight boost when it is paid. Unless you are getting the collector to agree to delete the item from your credit report with payment or you are getting a great settlement deal for 50 cents on the dollar, don't agree to pay it, and don't agree to new terms. Don't make any new deal or arrangements with the creditor, because (under the law) that would constitute activity and could restart the statute of limitations (SOL) for being sued on the account. They wouldn't be able to bring the date of first delinquency with the original creditor to the current date (which would illegally re-age the account and cause it to be reported for another 7 years) but they will be able to sue you for a longer period into the future should they decide to do so. As we learned earlier, all states have different statute of limitations terms when it comes to filing a lawsuit.

Furthermore, while the date of last activity (DLA) does not affect the credit score, the date of first delinquency does. Remember, the date of first delinquency is the date when the account holder first went delinquent for the series of delinquencies that led to the account being charged off. If, for example, the account holder paid 60 days late and then brought the account current and then afterwards went late again but this time the account was charged off, the date of first delinquency being reported would be the second time the person went late.

When full payment is made on a collection account, collection agencies update credit bureaus to reflect the account status as "Paid Collection." When this happens, the date of last activity becomes more recent. Sometimes errors occur in the updating process and the date of first delinquency is changed along with the DLA. This is an error that harms the score. Since recentness of a derogatory affects the score, and the credit scoring software uses the date of first delinquency, a recent payment on a collection account damages the credit score more severely if the collector inadvertently changes the date of first delinquency along with the DLA. This frequently occurring reality is certainly unfair, but it is something that must be worked around when trying to maximize your score. The score will not decrease if only the DLA is updated, but it is the sporadic occurrence of the date of first delinquency being updated that will reduce the score, so you need to be aware of this hazard.

Settling Collections: Best Practices

When we talk about settling collections, either you're 1) settling for deletion or 2) settling for the cheapest amount possible. Only collection agencies will give you a deletion in return for payment of the collection. The big banks and credit card companies will not delete the charged-off account or agree to remove past payments that were late in exchange for pay, so don't bother with that. With them, just get the lowest settlement amount possible. And don't let them intimidate you by saying that if you don't pay the account in full it will harm your credit score. The charge-off has already damaged the score, and the difference to your score between settling by paying in full or settling by paying less than the amount owed is only a few points, if any at all. It's just not worth paying the higher amount.

If you do decide to settle a collection, what is the best way to pay it and maximize your score? The best way to handle this credit scoring dilemma is to contact the collection agency and explain that you are willing to pay off the collection account under the condition that all reporting is withdrawn from credit bureaus. Request a letter from the collector that explicitly states their agreement to delete the account upon receipt/clearance of your payment. Although not all collection agencies will delete reporting, it is worth the attempt because the reward is great for the ones that do.

If they refuse to delete, it is usually because they say they are forbidden from deleting accurate information by the contract they have with the bureaus. The most effective response you can have in this case is to say that they did not properly notify you about the debt and that the initial reporting of the collection would not have occurred had you had the chance to pay them during the first 30 days after they sent the initial dunning letter. This very reasonable excuse, coupled with the fact that you are offering them 100 cents on the dollar, should be enough to convince most collectors that it is best that they accept your offer and delete. Keep in mind, though, that you should always offer 100 cents on the dollar when attempting to get a deletion. You are already making the collector feel that they are outside their comfort zone by requesting a deletion, so you need to make it worth their while in return or you risk their saying no.

Let's assume that after all of your negotiating the collector still says no to deleting with full payment. Then you want to switch gears and tell them that you are only willing to pay a percentage of the total amount due since they won't delete. Try to get 50 cents on the dollar, if you can.

As I've said, if you are not planning on settling your unpaid collections and charge-offs, the last thing you want to do is dispute them—especially if they are within the SOL for being sued! This is because your dispute itself can trigger them to channel their energy towards you, which may sometimes lead to the filing of a lawsuit against you, which would never have been filed had you quietly sat back and not rattled the tiger's cage.

Sometimes it's absolutely worthwhile to pay all or a portion of an outstanding debt if it will get a negative item removed from your credit report.

When It Works:

For accounts up to 4 years old, if you have the money, settle for deletion when you can. If you can't get the deletion, settle for the lowest amount possible.

If the account is more than 4 years old, but the SOL in your state is longer than 4 years, you may want to settle to avoid a lawsuit. However, even if the SOL has not run out, and the amount you owe is less than $1,000, I have found that the chances of a lawsuit are almost zero. In this case, I recommend not paying, as the account is so old it is not hurting the score that much. If you don't have the money, don't worry about it.

For accounts that are 6 years old, I don't care if you're the richest person in the world, don't pay them! At the 6-year mark, it doesn't make sense to pay because it won't increase the score much at all and the account will soon fall off the credit report.

Remember, it's very difficult to get a settled account removed after you've paid it, so you must negotiate it ahead of time. The goal is always to try to settle for deletion first, and if that fails, settle for the least amount possible then try to get it removed by dispute. If you don't settle an account and try to dispute it when there is a balance owing, even if you get it removed it will likely reappear. That's why it's best in the long run to settle.

How to Do It:

Step 1: Call the collection agency to make sure the information on the credit report is correct. Sometimes the collector will give you different information than what is being reported on your credit report. You'll need this information when trying to determine the expiration of the SOL or to help in negotiating a better deal. If they lack the information needed to prove that you either owe the debt or owe the amount they claim, you'll be in a much better bargaining position. You'll need to ask a series of questions, outlined below, to determine where you stand. Also, have your Social Security number ready and all of your account information in front of you. Call the collector with whom you are attempting to settle and ask:

- What is the total amount due? (Usually it is different from the credit report; sometimes it's even already paid!)

- What is the principal amount owed? How much is interest and fees? (Knowing this can be of benefit when negotiating how much to pay in settling. "It's not like people are losing money over there...")

- Who is the original creditor? (You want to know the chain of ownership on the account. You want to find out if it has been sold a few times because that increases the chance that the collector won't be able to prove that you owe the debt. If their records of who the original creditor was are incorrect, you can take advantage of that: If they don't know, you can get it deleted from the credit report because they don't have a way to prove the debt even belongs to you. In this case, you'll want to send a dispute letter to the CRAs with the dispute reason, "Not my account.")

- What is the date of first delinquency with the original creditor? (This is important because, with written contracts, this date determines when the statute of limitations is up. All states are different. The information they have may be different from what's on the credit report, so you need to know what they have in their records, to know if the SOL is up. This gives you bargaining power. If the SOL is up, they may have no other leverage to collect.)

> ➤ Date of Last Payment is when the last payment was received.

> ➤ Date of Last Activity can mean date of last payment or the last time you agreed to new terms.

• Was the account purchased by this particular collection agency, or is this collection agency hired to collect by the original creditor? (Was the account sold or assigned? If the latter, the collection agency has no power to make a decision on the account. If the former, before reporting you to the credit bureaus, the collection agency that purchased your debt must send you the dunning letter saying that you owe the debt and if you don't contest that fact within 30 days it will be considered an acknowledgement that you owe the debt.)

Step 2: If you can pay the collection in full, ask for deletion. If you can't afford to pay it in full, or they won't agree to delete, try to settle the debt for 35% to 65% of the amount owed. Please note that this strategy is for collections that are within the SOL and over $1,000, as these types of debts, if remaining unpaid, often lead to a lawsuit being filed before the statute expires. For debts that are within the SOL but are under $1,000, you're generally safe, as the amount to be collected is not worth the collector's effort and expense in filing a lawsuit.

If the collector refuses to delete in return for payment, they will usually try to tell you that deleting from the credit report is illegal. They're wrong. It's not illegal. It *is* a breach of their contract with the CRAs, but it's not illegal. They have an agreement with the CRAs not to delete items from the credit report in exchange for payment from the consumer. Tell them, "It's not illegal; it's against your contract with the credit bureaus, which has nothing to do with me." Then you need to give them a reason to think that what they are reporting is not accurate, and thus it's their responsibility to remove it; otherwise, it's unfair to you and against the FCRA. For example,

"I wasn't properly notified about it. Though I'm willing to pay it 100 cents on the dollar, you're not deleting it because I'm paying it but because I wasn't properly notified about it."

Argue the point that if you had had an opportunity to pay this debt in the first place, you would have paid it. The fact that you didn't receive their initial collection letter prevented you from paying it before it got on your credit report and therefore it is an error on their part and they should agree to delete after you pay them. Trust me, they won't argue too hard if they are getting 100% of what is owed and you are also giving them a reason to help you without their having to admit that they are violating their agreement with the bureaus. Sometimes they just won't agree to delete with payment, but if you can afford to pay the collection in full it is certainly worth a try.

If they do agree to delete with payment, ask them to put it in writing before you pay. Most of the time they'll agree to put it in writing but sometimes they'll refuse. Collection agencies have a couple of reasons for not wanting to send out letters that reference deletion or agreement to delete: First, they don't want these letters getting back to the CRAs since the bureaus might reprimand them for deleting accounts that might be accurate. Secondly, people often try to alter the letters in Photoshop. So, while they may agree to delete, and actually do the deletion, they may not issue a deletion letter. It may be luck, but I've never been let down by any collection agents who have agreed to delete.

Let's discuss the things you can do to best ensure that the account gets deleted in the event the collector doesn't want to give you a deletion letter but says they will delete once payment is made:

1. Ask them their name and extension and write it down along with the date and time so you can reference this information in future follow-up.

2. Ask them to notate the agreement to delete in the account notes.

3. Ask if you can write a restrictive endorsement on the back of the check, such as: "Cashing this check is an agreement to

settle in full and delete account # ____ from (Your Name)'s credit bureau reports." You need to get their permission on this because sometimes, with big agencies, the accounting department will see the restrictive endorsement and send the check back. If they say no to this, ask what else they can do to make sure the account gets deleted.

4. Write a letter and send it with the check, stating: "Please check the notes on this account. So and so at ext. XXX agreed to delete with payment. Here's the payment, so please delete." Then follow up by phone a week later to make sure they are planning to delete.

5. Cross your fingers and hope for the best!

The Two Types of Deletion Letters

There are two types of deletion letters you can get from a collection agency:

1. "Agreement to Delete letter": You get this before you mail the funds. Please note that you will still have to get the next letter from them once your payment has cleared in order to get it deleted from the credit bureaus.

2. Actual "Deletion letter": Provided after the collector has received your funds. Even if they don't issue this letter, you can still send in the previous letter along with proof that you paid the account and ask the bureau to delete the account, but it is just smoother if you can send an actual letter to the bureaus from the collection agency that states, "The account belonging to so and so should be deleted from the credit report." Keep in mind that this letter must reference the account number, your name, the fact that it should be deleted, be signed by someone at the company along with their contact information, and finally, be dated within the last 90 days. If the letter is older than 90 days, the bureaus will reject it.

Settling a Collection for Less Than Full Balance

If the creditor or collection agency won't agree to delete with payment or if you simply just want to get the best deal possible and don't care to pay extra for a deletion letter, the best approach is to give them an offer of around 30 to 40 cents on the dollar and see what they reply with. Always claim to be broke and that you have a family member who said they would help you if you can negotiate a good deal. If you end up paying 50 cents on the dollar or less in the end, you did very well. Make sure to get these settlement agreements in writing since there is no way to prove they agreed to accept less unless you have a document from them stating so.

Negotiating collections is not that hard to do, but you have to know what to say and how to educate the collector on how to help themselves. It's a cat and mouse game. When you know what to push and what not to push, you end up getting the most things removed.

Here are a few more tips: Don't bully them. They're just an underling. They are used to people calling all day long attacking them; if they do have the power to help you, they won't want to if you verbally abuse them. It's important not to be accusatory, and to develop a rapport. I have seen representatives pull an account out of internal charge-off because they wanted to help a client who was being humble, cordial, and sincere in asking for their help. Better to act dumbfounded at how you didn't receive the bill, or some other reason you're not at fault, than angry at them.

Always look for a flaw in their argument. Say, "I didn't screw up," but still trying not to blame them. Instead, try to blame a third party: the mail, that it fell off the conveyer belt at their offices, and so on.

On a side note, if you ever have to call a creditor or collection agency to settle an account but can't find the contact number for them on the credit report, first do a quick Google search for the company in order to find their website. If that fails, you can call the credit reporting agency of the credit report that has the collector listed and ask them for the creditor's phone number.

Settling Credit Card Debt

If you are current on your credit cards and want to settle them for less than what you owe, you'll need to stop paying the credit card company for about four to six months before the credit card company will be open to the idea of getting less than what you owe them. You can't settle for less than what you owe with the credit card companies until you're really late and your credit is already trashed. The 4-month mark is a good time to call to settle because that is when the creditor is starting to get nervous. Whenever you do call the big banks, if you are calling to settle the account after the SOL has run out, you should only be paying 30 cents on the dollar max since they can't sue you. But, when you're past the SOL and the account is at the 6-year mark and one year away from falling off, why pay anything, since it's not affecting the credit score that much? Save the money!

Also, be aware that, whether they actually inform you or not, the bank may report the forgiven portion of the debt to the IRS as taxable and send you a 1099. This is okay since the money you saved is considered a taxable benefit to you by the IRS.

Following Up

Whether you are settling a collection or settling a credit card with the bank, it is very important to follow up with them regarding whatever terms you agreed to because these settlements fall through the cracks more times than not. If you settled for deletion of a collection, make sure that they delete the account within the timeframe promised or call them if they fail to do so. Always check to see if they followed through with whatever you agreed upon.

WHO TO PAY FIRST TO MAXIMIZE YOUR SCORE

When you have limited funds and want to increase your score as much as possible, prioritize who you pay in the following order:

1. **Past Due Balances:** Accounts that are not currently 90 days late or more, charged-off, or in collections but have a past due balance should be paid first. A past due balance in the "past due" column on the credit report severely damages your credit score and should be the first accounts you pay. Paying only the past due balance on these accounts will bring the account current, and the past due status will go away within 30 days in most cases.

   If the account is already a collection, a charge-off, or even currently 90 days late or more, you do not want to pay the account first because an account in one of these statuses is already a major derogatory that is killing your score. Paying the past due balance on an account in these scenarios won't change the damage—the account will still be a major derogatory even after the past due amount is removed.

   Remember: This advice is assuming that you have limited funds and need to prioritize who gets the limited money you have and at the same time increase your score as much as possible. If you hit the lottery, pay everyone!

2. **Collection Companies That Agree to Delete:** The most recent collections showing on your credit report (that are more than $100 when initially reported[11]) that are willing to delete in return for payment should be the next place you spend your money.

---

[11] The reason I say above $100 when initially reported is because the newest credit scoring software from FICO does not score these accounts.

3. **Credit Cards:** If you have any money left over, pay down your revolving credit cards. Bringing down your revolving debt ratio increases the score a lot and paying these accounts as close to zero as possible is ideal. (We'll discuss this more in Chapter 5.)

4. **Settle Collections and Charge-offs That Won't Delete with Payment:** After you pay the revolving accounts, if you still have money left over, I would suggest settling the collection and charge-off accounts that won't agree to delete, with the most recent accounts in this category being settled first. Make sure you settle for as little as possible since having a fully paid collection or charge-off has basically the same effect on your score as a settled collection or charge-off. In fact, a paid charge-off/collection account may yield only one or two points more to your score, if any at all. Save the money and settle, the few points you'll gain is not worth the extra money.

5. **Tax Liens and Judgments:** These should be the last items you pay, as paying them will have almost zero effect on your score and may even *decrease* the score if a separate satisfaction document is filed with the court and appears on the credit report as a result of your paying it. The reason for this is that the credit score software will treat that separately listed satisfaction as an additional public record and cause the score to go down.

IDENTITY THEFT: HOW TO COMPLETELY ERASE THE NEGATIVE EFFECTS IN LESS THAN 10 DAYS

As we discussed in Chapter 2, identity theft is one of the fastest growing crimes in America today and it poses special problems for cleaning up your damaged credit report.

Identity theft occurs when someone uses your personal information such as your name, Social Security number, credit card number, or other identifying information without your permission to commit fraud or other crimes. The result is a credit report full of derogatories.

Most victims of identity theft spend hundreds of hours and sometimes years trying to rectify the negative credit rating that results from being a victim of identity theft. The good news is "you don't have to." If you follow the steps outlined below, your negative credit rating will be restored in most cases within 10 days. Be sure to keep a detailed record and copies of all correspondence.

Step 1: Place a fraud alert on your credit reports to help prevent an identity thief from opening any more accounts in your name. To do this, contact the toll-free fraud number of any of the three major credit bureaus (see below) and place a fraud alert on your credit report or send a letter requesting the same along with proof of address and proof of Social Security number. You only need to contact one of the three companies to place an alert because the company you call is required by law to contact the other two CRAs.

> **Equifax® fraud division**
> P.O. Box 740250
> Atlanta, GA 30374
> 1-800-525-6285
>
> **Experian® fraud division**
> P.O. Box 1017
> Allen, TX 75013
> 1-888-397-3742
>
> **TransUnion™ fraud division**
> P.O. Box 6790
> Fullerton, CA 92634
> 1-800-680-7289

There are three types of fraud alerts: 1) an initial alert, 2) an extended alert, and 3) for those on active duty in the military, an "Active Duty" alert.

• An initial alert stays on your credit report for at least 90 days.

- An extended alert stays on your credit report for 7 years. You can have an extended alert placed on your credit report if you've been a victim of identity theft and you provide the consumer reporting company with an identity theft police report and a notarized identity theft affidavit. In addition, the consumer reporting companies will remove your name from marketing lists for pre-screened credit offers for 5 years unless you ask them to put your name back on the list before then.

To place either of these alerts on your credit report, or to have them removed, you will be required to provide proof of:

1. Your Social Security number. (Either a copy of your SS card, a pay-stub, 1099, or W-2 will suffice. You only need one.)

2. Your mailing address. (A utility bill, bank statement, or signed copy of a lease agreement will suffice. P.O. Boxes are okay; it just needs to be your current mailing address.)

3. Your proof of identification in a picture I.D. format issued by a government entity (driver's license, state-issued I.D.).

- An active duty alert is available to persons on active military duty and is similar to an initial 90-day alert, except that it lasts 12 months and your name is removed from pre-screened offers of credit or insurance for two years.[12]

Step 2: File an Identity Theft Police Report with your local law enforcement agency. A simple one-page police report that states you were a victim of identity theft (with no other details) will suffice, although you should include the details, "if any," that you are aware of.

Step 3: Complete and get notarized an Identity Theft Affidavit. Complete instructions on how to complete this form plus the actual form itself can be accessed at *www.CreditMoves.com/identitytheft*.

---

[12] If you want to remove yourself from receiving pre-screened marketing offers, but you are not in the military or a victim of identity theft, simply go to *www.optoutprescreen.com* to remove yourself from these lists, or call 1-888-567-8688.

Step 4: Send the bureaus a copy of the police report, the notarized identity theft affidavit, a copy of your credit report with the fraudulent items circled (not needed but recommended), and a cover letter similar to the one below. Mail complete sets to all three credit bureaus and each fraudulent creditor account listed on your credit report. Make sure you call each creditor separately and ask them which address you should mail correspondence that pertains to your being a victim of identity theft. The Fair and Accurate Credit Transactions Act (FACT Act) requires that you obtain a specific address from each creditor in order to be protected by its provisions. Federal law also states that a creditor may also request that you complete one of their identity theft affidavits in their format, although most will accept the one mentioned in this book.

The credit bureaus have four business days to block the fraudulent information after receiving your request outlined in the steps above and also must prevent the fraudulent items from reappearing on your credit report.

Sending the information to the credit bureaus should do the trick by itself, but I highly suggest being diligent and putting the creditors on notice also in the event the credit bureaus don't do what they are supposed to.

Following are sample letters you will need to send to the CRAs and creditors. A sample of a blank Identity Theft Affidavit and an Identity Theft Affidavit with Instructions are available at *www.CreditMoves.com/identitytheft*.

Identity Theft Letter to the CRAs:

To: [All three CRA names]

[CRA addresses]

Today's date: _____

Re: Identity Theft Victim

To Whom It May Concern:

Please be advised that I am a victim of identity theft and that the fraudulent items listed below do not relate to any transaction that I made or authorized and are solely a result of Identity Theft. As required by [15 U.S.C. §1681c-2], I am including the following items:

- A government issued ID with a picture
- Proof of my Social Security number
- Proof of my address
- Identity Theft Police Report
- Identity Theft Affidavit "notarized"

In addition, I am including a copy of my credit report with the fraud items circled.

According to [15 U.S.C. §1681c-2], when a consumer provides the above listed items, the credit reporting agencies have four business days to block the fraudulent information from the time the request is received and also must prevent the fraudulent items from reappearing on the credit report. Please adhere to these mandated guidelines by removing the following fraudulent items that were a result of Identity Theft and send me a corrected copy of my credit report when you are finished doing so.

Sincerely,

Joe Consumer

Fraudulent Creditor Item	Account #
1. American Express®	371123349983333
2. ABC Collections	87683959603
3. Discover®	65412586562554

Identity Theft Letter to the Creditors:

To: [each creditor that has an account that was part of the identity theft]

Today's date: _____

Re: Identity Theft Victim

To Whom It May Concern:

Please be advised that I am a victim of identity theft and that the account I have with you with the account number listed below was a result of the fraud. I am including a copy of the correspondence I sent to the credit bureaus for your records.

Fraudulent Creditor Item	Account #
1. American Express®	371123349983333

Sincerely,

Joe Consumer

SECURITY FREEZE

A security freeze takes a fraud alert to a whole different level. A security freeze prevents almost anyone from pulling your credit report at all. You may want to add a security freeze if you really want to put your credit report on lockdown and make it much less likely that you'll be a victim of identity theft. If someone tries to pull your credit while a security freeze is active, your report will be blocked and the creditor won't get any information. There are limited instances where someone can obtain your credit report if you place a security freeze on it; those include: 1) the creditor is an existing creditor of yours, 2) you temporarily lift the freeze, or 3) there is a court order. Whether to place a security freeze on your file is a matter of personal preference that only you can decide based on how much protection you want against identity theft.

The cost of a security freeze ranges from free to $15, depending on your state and also whether or not you are already a victim of identity theft. Only you can request that a security freeze be activated on your credit file. You may place, temporarily lift, or remove a security freeze on your credit file under state law or through the bureaus' voluntary security freeze program. The security freeze will generally remain on your credit file until: 1) you request that it be removed, or 2) you request a temporary lift of the security freeze for a specific party or parties, or specific period of time, as applicable under state law or the bureaus' voluntary security freeze program.

If you choose to place a security freeze on your credit file, be sure to plan ahead if you are going to apply for credit. It may take up to three business days to process a request to temporarily lift a security freeze. Additionally, you may not be able to request a temporary lift of a security freeze during non-business hours or on weekends.

To determine the methods and fees for placing a security freeze or to request a temporary lift or remove a security freeze, see *www. CreditMoves.com/security*.

Submitting, temporarily lifting, or removing a security freeze request by mail requires that you submit the following information to the credit bureaus while keeping in mind that, unlike a fraud alert, you need to contact each bureau separately that you want to place the freeze with. Also remember that a security freeze will not auto-matically remove you from the pre-screened marketing list and you would still need to opt-out from receiving those offers by visiting *www.optoutprescreen.com*.

Below, I am going to go through the process needed to accom-plish putting a security freeze on your Equifax® profile. The instruc-tions and links to the bureaus' websites to accomplish the same for Experian® and TransUnion™ can be accessed at *www.CreditMoves. com/security.*

Equifax® Security Freeze Procedure

To Place a Security Freeze:

Send a letter via mail requesting that a security freeze be placed on your credit profile and include the below required personal ID infor-mation/proof and mail everything to:

> **Equifax® Security Freeze**
> P.O. Box 105788
> Atlanta, GA 30348

- Your complete name, including any suffix (e.g., Jr., Sr., etc.)

- Complete mailing address, Social Security number, and date of birth to the address above. (Make sure to include proof of address and Social Security number—i.e., driver's license or utility bill with your name and current address showing on it to prove address; a copy of your Social Security card, a 1099, a W-2, or a pay-stub with your Social Security number on it to prove your Social Security number.)

To Temporarily Lift a Security Freeze:

To temporarily lift a security freeze, you must submit all of the items listed above that were required to place the security freeze PLUS the following additional information:

- The 10-digit personal identification number (PIN) given to you after you placed the freeze

■ Include in your letter the date range, if your state allows for a date range lift (e.g., April 5, 2011 – April 12, 2011) for the temporary lifting of the security freeze or proper information regarding the third-party creditor you want to receive your credit report (e.g., American Express®), if your state allows for a third-party lift.

To Permanently Remove a Security Freeze:

To permanently remove a security freeze, you must submit all of the personal ID information required when you initially placed the security freeze plus your 10-digit PIN given to you after you placed the freeze, and state in your letter that you want the freeze permanently removed.

Charges for Security Freezes:

The charges for security freeze requests on your Equifax® credit file varies by state. These fees associated with your state's file freeze law can be accessed at *www.CreditMoves.com/security.*

Make sure to include your state's fee payment by check or money order for the appropriate fees.

If You Lose Your PIN:

If you lose the 10-digit security freeze personal identification number (PIN) provided to you when you placed the security freeze, you may request a new PIN for a fee prescribed by your state's law.

Experian® and TransUnion™

Rather than read through a similar explanation to that above of what is needed with Equifax®, if you want to place a security freeze on your Experian® or TransUnion™ credit reports, visit *www.Cred itMoves.com/security* to get the link directly to each of the other bureaus' websites where the freeze can be added.

TIME TO SUE:
WHAT TO DO IF ALL ELSE FAILS!

Imagine this scenario... You discover errors on your credit reports by one or more of your lenders. You challenge them and ask the credit bureaus to correct or remove them. Thirty days later the credit bureaus send you a reply confirming that what they have on file is accurate and it will not be removed or changed. They also direct you to contact your lender if you have any further questions regarding that allegedly incorrect credit reporting. You take the same course of action with the lenders reporting the incorrect information and, again, you are unsuccessful in getting the items corrected.

The scenario just described happens thousands of times every week. And while the Fair Credit Reporting Act (FCRA) is designed to protect consumers from credit bureau and lender negligence, the number of valid challenges to credit report data is not decreasing. Unfortunately, the number of challenges that result in credit reporting data being amended in favor of the consumer pale in comparison to the number that remain the same.

At this point you, the consumer, have two very simple options; you can either live with the erroneous information until the FCRA reporting period expires and the account falls off (normally 7 years), or you can escalate your efforts to have your credit reports corrected by filing a lawsuit.

Many experts are predicting an increase in consumer credit lawsuits due, in part, to consumers feeling the sting of increasingly difficult access to credit because of the credit crunch and a willingness to incur the costs of litigation to restore their good credit standing. To some people, it's an investment—do the math. If it costs you $20,000 in legal costs to force a lender or credit bureau to remove an inaccurate collection, and the removal allows you to qualify for a mortgage interest rate that saves you $100,000, you tell me, was that a wise investment?

In fact, it's possible that you'll recover all of your legal costs as part of a settlement if your case is strong. It seems logical that the credit bureaus would not prefer that a jury determine punitive damages in a case where they have sold credit reports to a lender that contained inaccurate information, but there is also a risk that the judge will grant only a portion or none of your attorney's fees and then you're out that part of the money. The tradeoff for the credit reporting industry is legal fees and a controlled settlement amount, versus the unknown of taking the case to trial where the odds are not certain that at least one of the members of the jury has not had a similar experience with a credit bureau or lender.

The credit bureaus are sued hundreds of times each year with the majority of those lawsuits being filed in Georgia, California, and Illinois. It's not a coincidence that the filings are disproportionate to those states given that's where the three national credit reporting agencies are based. The credit bureaus also maintain insurance against such lawsuits so the costs can be limited to premiums and deductibles in many cases. Having said that, it's certainly not a comfortable feeling knowing that you're about to go to war with a company large enough to easily absorb the cost of litigation.

So how do you know if you're prepared to sue your lender or one of the credit bureaus? Here's a checklist. If you can't answer yes to each of these, then litigation may not be for you.

1. Have you documented all of your calls with the lender and credit bureau? This means every conversation you've had with them since you started your attempts to have the errors corrected. This can be as simple as a handwritten summary of the conversation with dates and names.

2. Have you attempted to have the item corrected using the standard protocols? You can't simply file a lawsuit against the credit bureau without giving them the opportunity to correct their error. Be sure that you've exhausted your rights to challenge credit report items as defined in the Fair Credit Reporting Act.

3. Have you suffered any damages due to the incorrect item? If not, then think twice about filing a lawsuit. Damages can be credit declinations, credit approvals with disadvantaged

rates, higher insurance premiums, or the loss of a job due to credit report pre-employment screening. Can you document these things?

4. Can you tie the damages to the incorrect item? (Or are there other seriously negative items on your credit reports that are completely accurate that can be blamed for your damages?)

5. Do you have copies of your credit reports and FICO® scores and can you put together a chronology of credit reports and scores? If you can't, then you can subpoena the credit bureaus for archived credit reports and scores, although they will object profusely.

6. Are you absolutely certain that what's being reported is incorrect? Before you file a lawsuit, you need to do a reality check. If the items are accurate but simply not to your liking, save your money.

7. Does your case have a chance? An expert witness can assess this for you before you spend a dime on a lawyer and can give you an honest assessment of your chances for success and ways to better prepare for litigation.

CREDIT REPAIR:
HIRE AN EXPERT OR GO IT ALONE?

The Fair Credit Reporting Act provides numerous steps an individual can take to challenge negative items on their credit report. Unfortunately, while consumers have the ability to make these disputes on their own, as in most complicated issues, it is always best to have the advice of an expert to be as effective as possible.

A competent credit repair consultant should use a combination of sound advice their clients can act upon themselves in addition to helping clients remove inaccurate negative items from their credit reports.

The value of using a credit repair expert is that they do this every day, they know what works best and will give you the greatest likelihood of having inaccurate items removed. There's no guarantee, but they have years of trial-and-error experience to know how to get the best results. They know what strategies to use, the process for quickest results, and what language works best. Following is a brief list of how a credit repair expert can make a difference for you:

- no resistance or procrastination due to emotions
- knowing which items to dispute and which are a waste of time
- avoiding opening a new can of worms that can get you sued
- helping you spend your money where it will count the most toward a higher score
- representing you when you need to play hardball

Who Can't Credit Repair Help?

People with no money who have a ton of unpaid collections cannot be helped much by credit repair because whatever you do get removed from the credit report will just come back as the accounts remain unpaid. Sometimes money is the only solution and, without it, bankruptcy is the only path for seeing light at the end of the tunnel.

5

Other Strategies
for Improving Your Score

Much of Chapter 4 dealt with cleaning up negative credit items from your credit report. These items fall primarily in the first and fifth factors that make up the credit score: payment history and inquiries. But keep in mind that payment history and inquiries combined account for only 45% of what makes up your credit score. That being said, there are a few other huge areas that we can focus on to dramatically improve your score.

This chapter deals with the three factors that make up the remaining 55% of your credit score: debt utilization, length of credit history, and the types of credit used.

LOWERING YOUR REVOLVING UTILIZATION

As you know by now, your debt utilization ratio makes up 30% of your credit score. So let's recap what this category is all about.

What is revolving utilization? Simply put, it's the amount of credit you are using out of the total that's available to you. It's the debt you have in ratio to the total of your credit limits. It can also be viewed as the amount of purchasing power you have, calculated as the total revolving debt divided by the total revolving credit limits.

To calculate utilization on your revolving debt, add the credit limits together on all open credit card accounts, then add the balances together on all of these credit card accounts, and then divide the balance by the limit and multiply that number by 100. Credit utilization is expressed as a percentage. For example, if your credit available is $10,000, and your total debt is $5,000, then your credit utilization is 50%. Higher credit utilizations result in lower credit scores.

Ways to Lower Utilization

There are several ways to lower your utilization and improve your score.

1. Pay Before the Reporting Cycle

Most banks report your balance owed on the date your statement closes. If you are someone who pays off your balance every month, you will benefit by paying whatever you think you will owe at the statement closing date a few days before the statement actually closes so that the balance owed on the statement closing date is close to zero. Even if you max out the credit card the day after the statement closes, you will still have a zero balance for the next 30 days until the statement closes again, at which point it will report the balance owed on the closing date once again.

2. Pay Down Current Debt

A 3-digit credit score increase is possible when you pay off your revolving credit cards.

A maxed-out mortgage will not severely affect the credit score but a maxed-out credit card will. Pay off your credit cards as close to zero as possible and never close them because you want to have as much available credit as possible in order to have the lowest revolving utilization rate. If you close the credit card, you are taking away that available credit and your utilization rate will increase if you carry a balance.

3. Get Business Credit Cards

Even though you have to sign personally for the business credit cards, many business accounts don't get reported to your personal credit report unless you default. Given this fact, any debt you carry on business credit cards that do not report to the personal credit report will not hurt the score at all. If you transfer all of your personal credit card debt to a business credit card, you can increase your credit score dramatically even though you still have the same amount of debt.

4. Play the Transfer Game to Increase Your Available Credit

Transfer between credit cards to max out the card one month and pay it off the next month with another credit card. Transferring money back and forth between credit cards will make the credit card companies look at you like you're some Godfather by thinking you can handle the debt even though all you are doing is moving money from card to card. They increase your credit limits as a result. You can build a huge credit card portfolio and you'll always have money sitting at a very low interest rate since many of these balance transfers are at lower interest rates than the normal rate. But make sure you are aware that there is usually a 3% fee per transfer. Make sure not to do it too much if you are not ready to take the hit financially as a result of the transfer fees, but it is a great way to build credit over time.

I always advise my clients to have as high of credit limits as possible, so they have the best possible ratio of unused credit to credit limit. Asking for credit limit increases will decrease your debt ratio, ask every 6 months but be aware that you will incur an inquiry as a result but the end result usually justifies the means.

5. Use the Inactive Cards You Have

"We are writing to advise you about a change being made to your account." This prologue is a part of letters being sent to millions of U.S. consumers and sets an ominous tone for the remainder of the communication. The "change" being referred to is either your credit card account has been closed or the credit limit has been severely slashed. In this particular example, the credit limit was lowered on a Barclay's Bank credit card by $15,000.

In normal economic times a credit card issuer would only take such adverse action against one of their cardholders if they've done something wrong, such as miss a payment. However, millions upon millions of cardholders are seeing their terms changed because of seemingly innocuous actions such as "a change in spending patterns" or "inactivity." I guess we can attribute this to the fact that we're not in normal economic times, but it's not fair to consumers to leave it at that. Closing accounts and lowering credit limits can harm your FICO® credit scores. And since these actions are being taken against consumers who, in many cases, have fantastic credit scores, the damage can be dramatic. Here's what you can do…

Knock the dust off that old credit card – An inactive credit card, one that is open but never used, actually costs the credit card issuer money each month. Your account information is taking up space in their databases and they're still likely buying credit scores on you each month trying to decide how to entice you to actually use the card. If you never use the card, you are not generating merchant fees, or interchange fees, for the credit card issuer. And, obviously, if you're not using the card, you won't have a balance rolling month over month so you're not generating interest income for them either.

In many cases now, the issuer is simply choosing to lose you as a customer by closing your account. You want to avoid this, so you'll have to appease them by generating a little bit of revenue. The good news is that it won't come out of your pocket. Simply move the card to the front of your wallet and the next time you fill up your car or buy a pair of shoes, use that dusty credit card. This will reset the clock of activity and generate a little bit of income for the issuer. Pay off the bill when it shows up so you don't pay any interest and repeat this strategy at least once per quarter.

Watch your spending patterns – This is a friendly way of your issuer telling you that you don't have enough debt. For example, if you have a card with a $25,000 credit limit but have never charged more than a few hundred dollars in any month, and you pay it in full, then the issuer is questioning the need for such a high credit limit. They still have the risk of the "open-to-buy" (unused credit limit), so many have made the decision to adjust credit limits so they are more in line with your spending patterns.

Of course, to avoid this, you'd have to get into much more debt with that issuer, which could hurt your credit scores and cause other credit card issuers to take adverse actions too. If you've received a letter lowering your credit limits because of spending patterns, there's simply not much you can do other than be happy that they didn't close the account, which would have been worse. Continue to use the card sparingly and think about opening a new card to help replace the lost credit limit. Eventually we'll get back to the time when we can pay our credit cards on time and not have to worry about credit card issuers being scared of their customers, but for now you need to think outside of the box to prevent the bank from putting you outside of the vault!

Therefore, especially at this time where lenders are so wary, use all of your credit cards at least every few months. If you don't use your cards, they may close your account to cut their overall risks. If you have a HELOC (home equity line of credit), use it or you might lose it. They will be the first to go in this terrible market.

It's also important to keep paying down your cards so that creditors don't look at you as living off your cards and thus become more apt to lower your limit to mitigate their risk.

Remember that 15% of your credit score is determined by the age of the credit file. As you know, the credit scoring software from Fair Isaac[13] assumes people who have had credit for a longer time are at less risk of defaulting on payments. Therefore, even if your old credit cards have horrible interest rates, closing those cards will decrease the average length of time you've had credit once the account falls off your credit report since even positive credit will usually fall off the credit report once it is closed for 10 years. Keeping the card active is as simple as pumping gas or purchasing groceries every few months, then paying the balance down. The one thing all credit reports with scores over 800 have in common is a credit card that is 20 years old or older. Hold on to those old cards, trust me!

---

[13] Fair Isaac® is a registered trademark of Fair Isaac Corporation.

Full knowledge of your credit profile and how it represents you to creditors and credit bureaus is pivotal to full credit restoration success. Credit bureaus always advise individuals that they have a right to dispute their own credit files, but when the rights of the credit bureaus slow you down, you need to either know your stuff or know where to ask for help.

TYPES OF CREDIT YOU USE

If you've had a bankruptcy or otherwise destroyed your credit rating with charge-offs, collections, and other serious derogatories, you still need to get accounts to rebuild; otherwise, your credit will stay bad over time.

"Subprime" Cards

With bankruptcy, new subprime credit offers—those targeted at the riskiest credit population—will likely come right after your BK Petition is completed. This is because the banks know you are now out of debt and you can't file BK again for several years. Therefore, you are a moneymaker again in their eyes! Yes, the credit card offers will come, albeit with horrible rates and fees associated, but then again, you're in no position to negotiate. A couple of tips on these kinds of cards:

✓ make sure they report to the Big Three CRAs

✓ use them every month and pay on time for 6 months and then ask for a credit limit increase

✓ keep asking for credit increases as often as they become available

Secured Installment Loans & Secured Credit Cards

Building or rebuilding credit doesn't happen overnight. One of the quickest ways to start that recovery process is to deposit a couple thousand dollars into a savings account with a lender that will give you a secured installment loan or secured credit card against your money. This is not a risky loan for them because they have the amount of the loan held as collateral. You just borrow money (on an installment loan) or use the new credit card and make payments over time. The loan is reported to the credit bureaus like any other loan or credit card. If the loan is not paid back, the lender can seize the money in your savings account to offset their losses. Other common forms of collateral are automobiles, houses, stocks, and retirement accounts. A credit union is a good place to check to see if this type of loan is available.

LENGTH OF CREDIT HISTORY

This category may be the most difficult to improve, because only time heals here. What is important is to try to establish new credit accounts as quickly as you can and keep them open so that your accounts age from as early on as possible. The only way to speed this process is the authorized user (AU) route, but as we've discussed, the most recent version of FICO's Classic scoring model has safeguards built into the scoring software that bypasses most authorized user accounts for scoring purposes. Even though getting added as an authorized user probably won't help you due to the newer scoring models closing this loophole, I will still recap it here for those who want to give it a try in the event your credit report is scored by an older version of the scoring software or if you are lucky enough that FICO's newest software treats your authorized user account as one that they score.

AUs and FICO® 08

In previous scoring models, FICO® has given "authorized users" (AUs) credit toward their score. With FICO® 08 (the newest version of Classic FICO®), however, Fair Isaac® has changed their formula to prevent AUs from having their credit score improved by "piggybacking" on another account holder's good credit history.

This new version of FICO® apparently has the ability to determine if an authorized user credit card account is an attempt to game the credit scoring system through piggybacking, which is the process whereby a consumer with poor credit would pay to be added to the credit card of someone with good credit as an authorized user.

Fair Isaac® will not disclose how they're able to tell the difference between a legitimate authorized user account belonging to, say, a husband and wife versus one that has been made to a credit report through other means, such as piggybacking. FICO® 08 was originally going to completely ignore all authorized user accounts. This new logic seems to split the difference between ignoring all authorized user relationships and doing nothing to discourage the use of piggybacking services.

QUICK REVIEW & THINGS TO KEEP IN MIND

To wrap things up, I'd like to summarize some key things to keep in mind as you begin your credit repair adventure.

- If there are inaccurate items on your credit report, you will have to dispute them. You will need to contact the three major credit bureaus and dispute the accuracy of those items in order to force the credit bureaus and creditors to either admit or deny their accuracy.

- If your credit is beyond bad, it's going to take an epiphany on your part. You have to understand and accept that how you've managed your credit up to this point is exactly the opposite of how you should be managing it. You can't fake your way through this. It will require a significant change in your lifestyle and habits.

- The only way to improve your credit standing is to address the things that you are doing wrong. There is no blanket advice that anyone can give you that will work 100% of the time. Your recovery actions will be different from those of another person in the exact same situation.

- Your recovery plan will involve an initial purging of your current credit accounts. It's highly likely that you are using creditors who are more concerned about whether or not your next payment will ever arrive and less worried about helping you recover. The goal at the end of the day is for you to be able to pick and choose the lenders you like and have them fall over themselves trying to get your business.

- Unlike advice given by other so-called "experts," I believe your recovery journey should be taken head on—not by avoiding the issue. In fact, if you are discouraged and are planning on exiting the credit environment for more than 12-18 months, you might as well stop here. The only way to improve your standing is for you to jump right back into the credit world. Half your battle will be to convince not only your lenders and insurance companies but also the credit scoring models "through intelligent structuring of your credit profile" using the advice in this book that you are a new person. You can't do this if you try to live a credit-free life.

- Re-establish credit using any means necessary. You're not going to get the best rates initially, but that's okay. Keep in mind that it's only temporary. You have to build up your credit report with properly managed credit cards and loan accounts, and this is going to be costly.

- Once you're re-established, it's time to convert. It's when you'll be able to look your current lenders in the eyes and tell them to take a hike because they've just been replaced with better lenders. "Better," in this case, means unsecured credit cards with low interest rates and high credit limits and maybe even benefits like airline miles or cash back. It also means competitive rates and terms on car loans, mortgages, and insurance.

This recovery process should take less than 4 years. In fact, if you do it right, you should start enjoying credit products reserved for the elite even while you still have delinquencies on your credit reports. They don't have to be gone...but they do have to be a clear reflection of your PAST credit management skills.

Of course, if you don't have 4 years, you might want to find a quality credit repair expert.

Glossary & Acronyms

Account – An agreement between a creditor and consumer where the consumer purchases in such a way that causes the transfer of money from the consumer to the creditor over time.

Account Narrative – A comment on a credit entry that provides additional details about the entry or its status, which may or may not impact a credit score and may be added by a furnisher or a credit reporting agency.

Account Reviews – Inquiries on accounts where creditors have an ongoing relationship. (Not included in the business version of a consumer's credit report.)

Accrued Interest – Interest earned for the period of time that has elapsed since interest was last paid.

Affidavit – A voluntary statement taken under oath before a notary public, an officer of the court someone authorized to take.

AKA – Also Known As

APR – Annual Percentage Rate

Arbitration – Is a dispute settlement that is conducted outside the courts by a neutral third party and it may or may not be binding.

Asset – Items of value owned by an individual.

AU – Authorized User

Authorized – To give authority or official power to.

Automatic Stay – A bankruptcy provision that stops all creditor actions, including foreclosures, immediately upon a debtor's filing for bankruptcy protection.

Bankruptcy – A proceeding in a federal court to relieve a person or business of certain debts that the person or business is unable to pay.

BK – Bankruptcy

Breach – A violation or infraction, as of a law, a legal obligation, or a promise; to break or violate (an agreement, for example).

Chapter 7 – Under the federal bankruptcy code, this governs the process of liquidation for individuals or businesses. (The most common form of bankruptcy in the United States)

Chapter 11 – Under the federal bankruptcy code, this pertains to business reorganization.

Chapter 13 – Under the federal bankruptcy code, the debtor is able to keep possession of his/her property while under a court order repayment plan.

Charge Off – A debt that is considered uncollectible by the reporting firm and is subsequently written off.

Check Verification Companies – Provide businesses or individuals with the ability to check the validity of the actual check or draft being presented and the ability to verify the history of the account holder

Collection Agency – A firm that collects unpaid bills for other firms and is usually compensated by receiving a percentage of the amount collected.

Co-Maker – One or more persons who sign an instrument to indicate a promise to pay a financial obligation. (Also known as a Co-Signer.)

Communication – The conveying of information regarding a debt directly or indirectly to another thru thoughts, speech, writing or gestures.

Compliance – Conforming to a rule, such as a specification, policy, standard or law.

Consumer – Any natural person obligated or allegedly obligated to pay any debt.

Consumer Credit Counseling – An agency that helps debtors plan budgets and repay their debts.

Consumer Data Industry Association – The trade association for the nation's consumer reporting companies.

Consumer Statement – A personal statement that can be added to one's personal credit report to explain why a negative item is listed on the credit report.

Contract – An agreement between two or more parties that will be upheld by the law, either orally or in writing. To form a contract, the parties must be of the requisite age and mental capacity; there must be consideration and the subject of the promise cannot be illegal.

Co-Signer – One person who signs an instrument promising to back up a loan for somebody else.

CR – Credit Report

CRA – Credit Reporting Agency

Credit – A contractual agreement in which a borrower receives something of value and agrees to repay the lender at some later time.

Credit File – An ongoing record of a person's credit history based on information supplied by its creditors to a credit reporting agency.

Credit Score – A number based on an analysis of a person's credit files, to represent the creditworthiness of that person.

Creditor – Any person who offers or extends credit creating a debt or to whom a debt is owed, but such term does not include any person to the extent that he receives an assignment or transfer of a debt in default solely for the purpose of facilitating collection of such debt for another.

CROA – Credit Repair Organizations Act

DBA – Doing Business As

Debt – Any obligation or alleged obligation of a consumer to pay money arising out of a transaction in which the money, property, insurance or services that are the subject of the transaction are primarily for personal, family, or household purposes, whether or not such obligation has been reduced to judgment.

Debt Collector – Someone other than a creditor or its employees who regularly collects consumer debts on behalf of creditors.

Debtor – Someone who owes money to a creditor.

Default – Failure to perform or fulfill an obligation (Failure to make mortgage payments as agreed).

Deficiency Judgment – A court order stating that the borrower still owes money when the security for a loan does not entirely satisfy a defaulted debt.

Discharged – To relieve oneself of obligation, responsibility, burden or debt.

Duress – Unlawful constraint forcing one to perform an act to sign a document or instrument against his/her will.

ECOA – Equal Credit Opportunity Act

Equifax® is a registered trademark of Equifax Inc.

Execute – To make valid.

Experian® is a registered service mark of Experian Information Solutions, Inc.

FACT ACT – Fair and Accurate Credit Transactions Act

Fair Credit Billing Act (FCBA) – The federal law thats purpose is to protect consumers from unfair billing practices and to provide a mechanism to challenge incorrect information on credit accounts and address billing errors.

Fair Credit Reporting Act (FCRA) – A federal law that gives individuals the right to examine his/her credit report and correct errors and information used by credit reporting services.

Fair Debt Collection Practices Act (FDCPA) – A body of law that regulates the practices and behaviors of collectors and helps ensure proper and fair treatment for consumers.

Fair Isaac® is a registered trademark of Fair Isaac Corporation.

FCBA – Fair Credit Billing Act

FCRA – Fair Credit Reporting Act

FDCPA – Fair Debt Collection Practices Act

Federal Trade Commission (FTC) – The governmental agency that enforces and is responsible for monitoring and regulating the issues related to credit and consumer affairs in the United States.

FICO® is a registered trademark of Fair Isaac Corporation.

Foreclosure – The legal act taken by a creditor to force the sale of a property to satisfy a debt. Foreclosure occurs when a borrower has failed to make mortgage payments on a home. The borrower must vacate and the creditor sells the home to try to recover the money borrowed.

Garnishment – A legal proceeding in which a debtor's money, in the possession of another, is applied to the debts of the debtor.

Grace Period – An additional period of time past the due date in which a payment can be made without incurring a penalty and is not considered delinquent (example: mortgage, insurance, etc.).

HELOC – Home Equity Line of Credit

Inquiry – A request for access to a consumer's credit history made through a credit reporting agency.

Joint Debt – Two parties enter into a credit contract with equal repayment responsibilities.

Judgment – A legal decision per court order to pay or fulfill a financial obligation to another party.

MCAW – Mortgage Credit Analysis Worksheet

Mini Miranda Warning – Each time a debt collector contacts a consumer, he/she must give what is known as a "Mini Miranda Warning" containing the following words (or words imparting this meaning): "Hello, I am _____(Name of Collector). I am (or this office is) a debt collector representing _____ (Creditor). Information obtained during the course of this call/interview will be used for the purpose of collecting the debt."

myFico® is a registered trademark of Fair Isaac Corporation.

Per Annum – Yearly, annually.

Per Diem Interest – Interest calculated per day.

Public Records – Refers to proceedings or events recorded in courts that are open to the public (example: bankruptcies, divorces, garnishments, liens, or judgments).

Reinstatement – The payment of money sufficient to satisfy all amounts past due, including reasonable fees and costs incurred as a result of a default on a loan.

Released – A term assigned to a state or federal lien that has been paid.

Rescind – To withdraw an offer or contract.

RMCR – Residential Mortgage Credit Report

Satisfied – A term assigned to a judgment that has been paid.

Signature – The act of putting one's name on an instrument.

SOL – Statute of Limitations

Statute – An established law or rule.

Statute of Limitations (SOL) – Any law that places a time restriction during which a lawsuit must be brought to court or a crime must be prosecuted.

Subpoena – A legal process used to require the appearance of a person or documents into court.

Tax Lien – A debt attached against property for failing to pay taxes.

Terms – The amount of monthly payment or the number of months or years a loan is scheduled for repayment.

TransUnion® is a registered trademark of TransUnion LLC.

Usury – The illegal practice of lending money and charging a rate of interest greater than the maximum permitted by law.

Valuable Consideration – Type of promised payment upon which a promisee can enforce a claim against an unwilling promisor.

VantageScore® is a registered trademark of VantageScore Solutions LLC.

Void – Having no legal force or effect; not legally binding or enforceable.

Waive – To relinquish, abandon or forego a right to enforce or require something.

zendough® is a registered trademark of TransUnion Interactive, Inc.

Acknowledgments

Thanks go to:

All of the wonderful people with whom I've had the pleasure of working, throughout my career.

Ed Jamison, for giving of his time, talents and support to me over the years.

John Ulzheimer: your knowledge of the credit industry and mentoring has inspired me.

And finally, to my wonderful wife Jamie Minor, for no matter where I was or what I was doing, she has always supported my passions and believed in me. Words cannot express my gratitude and love.

About the Author

Doug Minor is an accredited expert on credit and mortgage issues. He speaks to audiences that include consumers, real estate and mortgage professionals, attorneys, accountants, and students. Doug has been featured on the CBS Channel 2 News, and quoted in articles appearing in FoxBusiness.com, Yahoo! Finance, and *Entrepreneur Magazine*. Doug is also in demand nationwide, as an expert witness and litigation consultant, with specialized expertise in the *Fair Credit Reporting Act* (FCRA) and Quantifying Credit Damages. His clients in this arena include major law firms representing consumers as well as lending institutions. Through his company, Easy Credit Relief, Inc., Doug provides a range of consumer services including credit repair, credit monitoring, identity theft recovery, divorce recovery, and credit & financial coaching.

Doug entered the mortgage field in the 1980s and enjoyed a successful career in both residential and large-scale commercial lending. He noticed that many of his clients desperately needed guidance, especially in the areas of credit management and repair. This led Doug to begin counseling people in credit use and responsible fiscal management, which soon became his primary occupation. Upon founding Easy Credit Relief, Inc., Doug developed the Credit Scoring Mortgage Analysis Model that has helped many of his clients. He also prospered investing in real estate, stocks, bonds and other more exotic transactions, personally applying the principles that he teaches to others. Through his writings and personal appearances, Doug shares the unique understanding of credit and money management that have propelled his success.

Doug Minor has a certification in the Fair Credit Reporting Act (FCRA) from the Consumer Data Industry Association (CDIA). He has been a licensed real estate salesperson, appraiser, notary public, and certified Divorce Planning Professional. He has also been certified by the Certified Mortgage Planning Specialist Institute in the fields of mortgage planning, cash flow management and real estate equity management.

Doug lives in Westlake Village, California, with his wife Jamie and their two children.

For a one on one consultation with Doug e-mail dougminor@easycreditrelief.com or call his office at 800-679-1505. For the most current information, follow him on Twitter or sign up for his credit updates on one of his websites: www.easycreditrelief.com , www.creditdamagesexpert.com , and www.dougminor.com